THE GENESIS
OF
EVOLUTION

THE GENESIS
OF
EVOLUTION

HOW GOD CREATED DARWINIAN
EVOLUTION IN SIX DAYS

ROGER WILLIAMS

BALBOA.
PRESS

A DIVISION OF HAY HOUSE

ISBN: 978-1-4525-6465-4 (sc)
ISBN: 978-1-4525-6466-1 (e)

Balboa Press books may be ordered through booksellers or by contacting:

Balboa Press
A Division of Hay House
1663 Liberty Drive
Bloomington, IN 47403
www.balboapress.com
1-(877) 407-4847

Because of the dynamic nature of the Internet, any web addresses or links contained in this book may have changed since publication and may no longer be valid. The views expressed in this work are solely those of the author and do not necessarily reflect the views of the publisher, and the publisher hereby disclaims any responsibility for them.

The author of this book does not dispense medical advice or prescribe the use of any technique as a form of treatment for physical, emotional, or medical problems without the advice of a physician, either directly or indirectly. The intent of the author is only to offer information of a general nature to help you in your quest for emotional and spiritual well-being. In the event you use any of the information in this book for yourself, which is your constitutional right, the author and the publisher assume no responsibility for your actions.

Any people depicted in stock imagery provided by Thinkstock are models, and such images are being used for illustrative purposes only. Certain stock imagery © Thinkstock.

Printed in the United States of America

Balboa Press rev. date: 12/07/2012

This book is dedicated to the creationists and evolutionists who treat each other's thoughts, statements, and writings with respect.

Contents

Contents

List of Qur'an Quotations in Sequence

For the sake of clarity, the names and pronouns used to address divinity will be capitalized.

I

The Creation Paradox Can Be Resolved

How God created Darwinian evolution in six days is revealed by the resolution of the creation paradox. So, we will resolve the creation paradox.

We will do this in a way that maintains the credibility of the Bible and the validity of scientific theories. The resolution of this paradox uses the premises and conclusions of the creationists and the evolutionists, and synthesizes the Bible's version of the creation with the fact supported theories of evolution and cosmology.

Once the resolution of the creation paradox is accepted, religious persons and scientists should be able to converse with each other about the origin of mankind without being concerned about a rejection of their beliefs.

1. Take a "Can Do" Attitude When Resolving Paradoxes

Although this chapter is not about the nature and resolution of paradoxes, it does look at three routine paradoxes to show that they can be resolved or shown to be nonsense. If we use comprehensive contexts, have enough pertinent knowledge, and avoid the abstract conundrums that protect them, paradoxes will cease to baffle us.

A "can do" attitude is needed to resolve paradoxes. We need to see ourselves as confident investigators of abstract thought processes. When we believe we can dismantle the abstract conundrums that protect paradoxes, the means to resolve paradoxes or show that they are nonsense will be discovered.

Even though we do not always have enough knowledge today to provide a final resolution for some paradoxes, we can still identify what we need to know to determine how a selected paradox can be resolved.

Before we proceed with our paradox resolution exercises, we will peek at the creation paradox in the next section.

2. What Is the Creation Paradox

The knowledge we will use to resolve the creation paradox is from our culture, the Bible, and science.

The creation of everything from nothing is the creation paradox. Everything and nothing are concepts that cancel meaning when one is used in the place of the other. To say one is the same as the other is contradictory and dismissive of the definition of words and their associated concepts. In practice, making something into nothing or nothing into something is impossible. One of the laws of nature important to the way our quantitative world functions is the law of the conservation of matter and energy. This law proscribes the reduction of matter and energy into nothing, and it also proscribes the creation of matter and energy from nothing. The resolution of the creation paradox includes this law. God's supernatural powers created this paradox by creating everything from nothing in spite of the law of the conservation of matter and energy. Did God violate the laws He created? He did not – as we shall see in later chapters.

Since the creation of everything from nothing is an expression of God's will, the authors of the Bible and Qur'an believed His will is what operates His creation. For these authors there is no creation paradox – just God's will.

But God did create natural laws to govern nature. He kept supernatural influence out of the operation of these laws. The authors of the Bible and the Qur'an were unaware of natural laws and why God created them free from the influence of supernatural powers. Supernatural powers were sequestered in the dwelling of spirits. The Bible called this place: the heavens. Today we call this supernatural world: heaven, hell, the other side, etc.

The author of the book of Genesis (some doctrines identify Moses as its author) did not explain why God configured His creation as He did. This is probably because God's will was viewed as inscrutable. People were not expected to understand anything that originated from an infinite source.

During the time the story of the book of Genesis was told and written, rulers were despotic, absolute, and could not be challenged by their subjects. The law of the tribe, kingdom, or empire was the ruler's will. If the ruler ordered the construction of a building no one asked him for a logical explanation. Since God was the ultimate ruler, His subjects did not ask Him questions about His creation just as they avoided asking their mortal rulers questions about their decrees. No one wondered about the creation paradox.

Before the creation of spirits and their world, the Creator's thoughts were about Himself, nothing, and the nature of everything (yet to be created). When thinking about various kinds of everything, fantastic fiction and what was to be real were mixed and were indistinguishable one from the other. The absolute flexibility of operation and content of fantastic fiction acquired essence and existence within the supernatural world. To give the occupants of the supernatural world a sense of essence and existence, the Creator dressed their environment with a semblance of place, movement, structure, and atmosphere. In spite of this accommodation by the Creator, there was still no limit and no distinction between the supernatural world and fantastic fiction. In this unlimited environment there were no paradoxes – and no creation paradox.

This extraordinary condition ended after the creation of the natural world. When our world and its laws of nature were created, the limits and distinctions between what was supernatural and what was real were also created. Within a world of structures, quantities, and rules, the creation of everything from nothing became a paradox.

All paradoxes were made by the Creator. So was the potential to form abstract ideas and concepts – real or fictitious. Abstract ideas and concepts which are not appended to what is real, exist in a world of fiction or metaphysical fiction. Because of the kind of creation

chosen by the Creator, the creation paradox is configured with a mixture of what is real, what is supernatural,
and what is fictitious. To resolve the creation paradox all
three of these domains of thought must be perceived and
integrated.

Whether or not the resolution of the creation paradox is established in this book will be determined by the
viability of its presentation in the arena of philosophical
and theological debate.

In the next section we will look at some of the elements
of the logical structure of paradoxes. Afterward, the rest
of this chapter will be devoted to resolving three routine
paradoxes.

In the remaining chapters our investigation will resolve
the creation paradox. During this process the Godhead
paradox (the three divine beings combined into a single
divinity) is resolved as well.

The last chapter will also explain why the creator was
motivated to configure the whole of creation as He did.

3. A Look at the Elements of Paradoxes

The word 'paradox' was adopted from part of the Greek
word 'paradoxon'. 'Para-' means beyond in Greek, and
'-doxon' means opinion (what one thinks). Today a
paradox means a statement which produces contradictory and absurd thoughts but which may nevertheless
be true when stated in a sensible manner. We are aware
of paradoxes because our minds are able to synthesize

contradictory or mutually exclusive concepts into abstract systems of thought that produce absurd relationships among the relevant concepts. The resolution of these entangled thoughts often requires an analysis technique and amount of knowledge not available to those that presented their paradoxes to the world. The discoverers of these paradoxes were not aware of the thought traps that had ensnared their perceptions. The hidden assumptions they had accepted when they presented their paradoxes kept them baffled.

Today, language, reason, mathematics, and the logical relationships among sets of concepts and sets of things are well developed. Yet, when paradoxes are presented to the members of our modern culture, many avoid investing their time and energy into a search for their resolution. Who can blame them? Our culture does not teach people how to deal with paradoxes.

Paradoxes are abstractions. Some appear to be appended to elements of reality, some are caught in a web of logical method and the use of language, and some are complex metaphysical fiction. The cause and effect paradoxes defy reality. The supernatural paradoxes dismiss natural laws. The logical systems of thought and the language paradoxes make absurd statements that appear truthful. All paradoxes raise questions about the validity of logical methods of analysis and the use of language to express rational thought.

We now turn our attention to the three routine paradoxes that we mentioned earlier. This exercise will show that paradoxes can be resolved. Once we see that the resolution of paradoxes is feasible, we will be able to proceed with the expectation of finding a resolution of the creation paradox.

4. A Look at the Statement Paradox

"This statement is false." This is the statement paradox. It is known throughout academic campuses. After the presentation of this statement, the question is asked: "Is this statement true?" The question focuses our attention upon the paradox. If the statement is true, then what it says about itself is not true. If the statement is not true, then what it says about itself being not true is not true. Further logical analysis adds to the confusion.

On the falsehood side of the paradox, we first accept the statement's claim that it is false. Being a false statement is then the truth about itself. But if it is stating the truth, then what it says about itself cannot be true. This is the contradiction on the falsehood side of the paradox.

On the truthful side of the paradox, we first accept that the statement about itself is made in good faith and is therefore true. The problem then confronts us that if the statement is true, then what it says about itself is not true. In this case the statement states the truth about its falsehood. But it then acquires the status of a paradox by being true as a statement yet false when it speaks of itself.

In both of these approaches, the statement is both true and false – a paradox.

This statement will remain a paradox as long as we

choose to allow ourselves to accept the limited context within which the paradox was spawned. One part of this context is the belief that the proper use of language will determine the truthfulness or falsehood of abstract ideas and concepts.

The use of language is practical. Language evolved to communicate what is true, but did not evolve to determine the truth. Language developed through a trial and error process while it supplemented nonverbal communication according to the needs of groups of people who shared a culture. While language could express truths and falsehoods about things and circumstances, the nature of these things and circumstances had an essence which was independent from the use of language. The environment that was external to the human mind remained unaffected by the use of language.

As language evolved to express the thoughts of people preoccupied with solving the problems of life, statements that referred to themselves were viewed as irrelevant oddities. If one used the statement, "This statement is false." to refer to the value of another statement different from itself, then it had the practical use of dismissing falsehoods and errors. No one expected such statements to refer to themselves. Except for moments when people played with language, self-referenced statements were useless.

One of the assumptions of the statement paradox is that language can be managed in a way that is similar to mathematics to determine truthfulness or falsehood. Mathematics can do this because it is involved with quantities. Involvement with quantities is but one very small part of the use of language. Nevertheless, the belief that the management of language will produce abstract facts the way this is accomplished by mathematics persists -- and does deserve to be tested, but tested in the broadest possible context. To evaluate the value of a statement, the context of the analysis must be free from thought constraining assumptions and elaborate self-enclosed systems of thought.

Self-enclosed systems of thought are useful for the evaluation of facts and beliefs that exist within the limits of their context. However, beyond the boundaries of their context, self-enclosed systems of thought are not qualified to determine the truthfulness or falsehood of a fact or belief. This becomes evident when the self-enclosed systems of thought become helpless when they are confronted by paradoxes of their own making. This happens because of the containment of the self-enclosed system of thoughts within 'thought rooms' that have no windows, doors, periscopes, electronic media, or other means to perceive outside of the boundaries of their self-enclosed contexts. In our culture today, we call these 'thought rooms' boxes in which thinking is trapped. Paradoxes are not resolved by trapped thinking.

Once we are free from the thought traps that accompany the statement paradox we can find a path to its resolution.

Let us look at the meaning of the statement. We know the statement refers to itself, but what does it state within the context of our real world? It states the truth of its being false, and since it is false, it states that any application of the truth to itself is false. So we know the statement is concerned about its truthfulness or falsehood. We are not aware of the statement's veracity status, and we are not aware of the subject matter within the statement.

If the statement is true and false, then what is it true and false about? What is the content of the statement? Where can we find its content? Statements that are a sentence have a subject; but this statement is its own subject.

Within the sentence of the statement paradox there is no content. The meaning of the statement cannot be found because there is nothing inside the statement.

The statement is its own subject, and that subject is void of content. The statement paradox is a statement about nothing. The subject of the statement is itself, and itself is nothing, so the statement is about nothing.

What the statement says is: "Nothing is false." The implication of nothing being false is that everything is true. Through the experiences of life, we know that some statements are true and some statements are false. Our statement is then a kind of fiction: it is couched as if it is speaking about something that is real, but it is speaking about nothing. In itself, the condition of being nothing is void of any value – positive or negative -- that can be determined to be true or false.

A mathematical expression of: "This statement is false." is $0 = \neq$ (zero is equal to not equal). This is evident nonsense.

"This statement is false." – the statement paradox -- is a misuse of language. To grant meaning to the self-referenced: "This statement is false." is to elevate verbal nonsense to the value level of sensible statements.

5. A Look at the Supernatural Powers Paradox

The supernatural powers paradox is about faith in the idea that to God all things are possible. After we read this section we will have the knowledge and perspective needed to resolve the supernatural powers paradox.

This paradox is presented by a question. "Since God can do anything, can He create a rock that is too big for Him to lift?" The presuppositions in this paradox are that God is omnipresent, omniscient, and omnipotent. Therefore, He can create and lift a rock that cannot be lifted. This paradox was designed to illustrate that God can do the impossible.

The supernatural powers paradox stifles logical thinking about the relationship that supernatural powers have with our world. This is convenient for anyone who wants to shut down our analytical scrutiny of God and His powers. The problem is, if we stop thinking about God, then the religious leader will do all of our thinking for us (and not just about God). Do we want this kind of relationship with the advocate of our religion? The consequences may be adverse to our existence. So, since God is also a thinker, let us think along with Him and agree or disagree with the leaders of our religion. Always assume that the thinking of the leaders of our religion is no better than your own – except in particular cases when he or she has shown us a better idea. You will find, however, that the leaders of religions have no ideas which can be used to resolve the supernatural powers paradox.

In the world we live in God must void the natural laws of gravity and inertia before He creates the big rock.

Otherwise, a rock of enormous size will cease being a rock and will collapse under its own force of gravity into a black hole similar to those located at the center of our galaxy. Free from gravity and inertia the largest rock God could create would be weightless. Even a baby could lift this weightless rock. God can always create a rock He can lift. Can He create one he cannot lift?

To find the rock God cannot lift, we ask Him to create a rock that is weightless, free of inertia, and infinite in size. After God has fulfilled this request, He has established the conditions necessary for the resolution of the supernatural powers paradox. To understand these conditions, we must review the nature of infinity.

In mathematics infinity is a value that is greater or lesser than any assigned value. In general, infinity is a concept of an absolute amount or state which exceeds any particular quantity or state. Included in states that can be infinite are flexibility, adaptability, elasticity, plasticity, rigidity, influence, modification, and constraint. Included in kinds of infinite quantity are length, area, volume, time, matter, energy, and force.

The nature of one kind of infinity is different from the nature of any another kind.

What all infinities have in common is that they cannot be made more extreme. An infinite amount or state is absolute. Each kind of infinity includes all the increments of its kind. Before a kind of infinity is reached, an amount or state of its kind can be added to its total. Once infinite, that particular kind of infinity cannot be increased. The human mind can always perceive an amount of infinity that is greater than its current perception of infinity, but this is an exercise in fictitious thoughts. What the mind thinks has zero effect upon the nature of infinities.

Knowing this about infinity we ask God to lift the infinite sized rock within the confines of our natural world – our world of quantitative relationships. God agrees. He attempts to lift the rock, and fails. (Of course, He knew He was going to fail.) The rock is immobile, so He has indeed succeeded in creating a rock that He cannot lift. The paradox is resolved. How?

The space-time continuum is filled by the rock. Where there was an infinite vacuum, there is now an infinite in size rock. There is no empty space left.

Since there is no space left, that is, there is no room left in which one can move, then there can be no motion. The rock cannot be moved up or in any other direction. The rock cannot be moved, so it cannot be lifted. God has created a rock that He cannot lift. To think otherwise is to indulge in fictitious thoughts.

A mystic will object to this evident failure of omnipotence in our world. He will say that God can create more space beyond infinity to move the rock. However, this cannot be done because God has placed a supernatural spell on the rock which keeps it infinite in size. He has done this because we asked Him to create an infinite in size rock. If He creates more space around the rock, the rock augments and fills the new space. This is because both the rock and space share volume as a kind of infinity. When they are both infinite, they are identical in size. The rock is not infinite in size when there is any open space beyond its surfaces.

Infinity adds to itself whenever a condition exists

which causes it to be less than what is required by its definition. If there is any space left for the rock to move, then it would not fit the definition of infinity. Many people modify, distort, and reject the definitions of words when those definitions interfere with the consistency and beauty of their fiction contaminated systems of thought. The human tragedy here is that once we ignore the definitions of words and symbols, the thoughts we try to communicate to another are modified, distorted, or fictitious.

One of the reasons mystics have difficulty in accepting limits to God's omnipotence in our world is that in their minds they mix events in the natural world with happenings in the supernatural world. But God's mind is not like the minds of mystics. It is safe to say that God is a rational supernatural being. He had rational reasons for setting up the creation as He did. The natural world's operations are limited by quantitative interactions. The supernatural world has no quantities and no limits. The supernatural barrier keeps the two worlds separated.

God can choose to intervene and recreate a portion of His creation. When He does, He has the power to convert what He imagines into what is real. The mechanism He uses is to envelop, for an instant, the objects of His intervention with a spirit extension from the supernatural world. When this happens, He makes changes to quantities which can be assimilated by the natural world. He has proven He wants a stable natural world and will not interfere with its quantitative nature. So, in our world the supernatural powers paradox is resolved.

The quantitative nature of our world is the reason the supernatural powers paradox has a resolution.

Nevertheless, this paradox does persist within the contexts of self-enclosed systems of thought. It is also viable within the boundaries of the supernatural world – the world of spirits.

The supernatural world has zero dimensions, is without chronological time, is free of all cause and effect relationships, has no natural laws, and has no actual quantitative infinity. The supernatural world has its own laws, and they are not anything like our natural laws. The laws of the supernatural world govern spirit beings and spirit symbols. Spirit symbols represent every individual thing – spirit, real, and fictitious. Spirit symbols are the embodiment in a spirit form of the essence and existence of each item of the creation -- real or otherwise.

In the spirit world, God can create a spirit symbol of an infinite rock. To this He can attach a spirit symbol of an infinite space-time continuum. Then He can attach the spirit symbol of Him lifting an infinite in size rock in an infinite space. He would be lifting them both at the same time in His world of spirits. This will perpetuate this paradox in the world of spirits, just as it is perpetuated in self-enclosed systems of thought. For the paradox to be perpetuated in our world, God would have to be an irrational and capricious divinity. By the nature of the universe He has created, we can see that He is neither irrational nor capricious. Our world has sensible quantitative cause and effect relationships; it does not have the features of fictitious thoughts; and it does not have the unlimited contortions of the world of spirits.

6. A Look at the Irresistible Force and the Immovable Object Paradox

The paradox of the application of the irresistible force against the immovable object has been on the minds of thinkers since the time of the ancient Greeks. Until the twentieth century there was never enough knowledge to provide a direction of thought that would resolve this paradox. Today we have enough knowledge to determine which theory we need to verify to find its resolution.

An irresistible force must have the capacity to become infinite in many directions or in one direction. The application of the force must adjust to fit the size of the immovable object. To be immovable, the object must have the capacity to produce a reaction force that is equal to the applied force and opposite in direction. This means the object's reaction force must be capable of reaching its infinity. The surface of the object must apprehend the applied force on one of its sides. The other sides of the object must be free from the applied force. Under the surface, the object's structure must be able to counteract the applied force with the reaction force. Even if the object became a liquid, a gas, or plasma, the reaction force must oppose the applied force.

To illustrate the physical effects of the two forces on the object, we will describe the increments of the applied force in seven stages. At each stage, the applied force increases when the object fails to move. During these increases of applied force there is never a fluctuation of the applied force. At the end of the seventh stage, the applied force and the reaction force reach their infinities.

Before the application of the irresistible force, the object can be of any size and shape, and it can be made of any kind of matter. The states of its matter can be solid, liquid, gas, or plasma. Our arbitrary choices for the object's shape, material, and mass are: a solid sphere, platinum, and one metric ton.

The effect upon the object, by the applied force and the reaction force, is compression. While the object is being compressed, it will diminish in size and remain a sphere.

When the applied force meets one side of the object's surface, its application is transferred to the interlocked platinum atoms. Each of the platinum atoms has a cloud of circulating electrons in its outer zones. At the center of an atom's nearly empty inner zone, a heavy micronucleus is lodged. The fast circulating electrons form the atomic shell of each of the object's atoms. These shells are like spherical springs that push back against pressure. The reaction force uses the atomic shells to counteract the applied force. The compression of the platinum atoms toward each other is the effect of the first stage of the application of the irresistible force.

In the second stage, the applied force increases until the compression causes heat. The object's temperature increases until it melts. After the object becomes white hot it becomes a liquidlike ball of gas.

During the third stage the object retains its shape, but it decreases in size. The applied force focuses its application to match the size of the object. The atoms are pressed so close together and under so much pressure, the atomic shells collide and knock their electrons out of orbit. As the electrons abandon their orbits, the atomic shells evaporate. Energetic x-rays flung by the hot electrons convert some of the compression forces into radiation. The object has now become a small bright ball of plasma constituted of electrons, photons, and the nuclei of the former platinum atoms. There is no production of fusion energy, as is produced in the core of our sun, because the nuclei of platinum atoms had already been fused billions of years earlier.

In the fourth stage of compression the platinum nuclei collide with so much violence it is their turn to knock each other apart. Refusion occurs when some of the smaller pieces of the former platinum nuclei interact, but the energy thus released is not sufficient to halt the continued compression. Soon the products of the refusion are themselves torn apart. As the forces increase, the dismantling of the atomic nuclei adds various kinds of particles (such as neutrinos) and high energy gamma rays to the object's spectrum of radiation. The miniscule ball of plasma now consists of fast moving protons, neutrons, electrons, and high energy photons.

During the fifth stage the compression the object's loose particles come together to eliminate most of the space between them. The space-time continuum around the object develops a sharp curvature. Gravity begins to assist the applied force with additional contraction. Electrons combine with protons to form neutrons. Mesons and other exotic particles wink in and out of existence. Most of the radiation produced is energetic gamma rays. The object's composition has become a roiling plasma made of neutrons that have no space between them. (The constituency of neutron stars is the same.) The activity of the neutrons is sufficient to increase the object's mass. The object has become an unstable ball of plasma smaller than a platinum atom.

In the sixth stage the collisions of the neutrons are so violent they breakup into their constituent quarks (three per neutron). The combination of the applied force, the reaction force, and the force of gravity is so great the object has become a miniature black hole smaller than a proton. The power of the combination of the three forces on the object is greater than the strong force. The object's quarks fail to maintain any combinations. All of the object's particles, elementary or otherwise, are either loose in a plasma soup or in orbit just below the black hole's event horizon.

The final increment of the applied force occurs during the seventh stage. The applied force increases until it has reached its infinity. At infinity, the applied force is irresistible. The immovable object's equal and opposite reaction force reaches its infinity while it matches the applied force. The force of gravity within the object does not reach infinity, but if you were inside the object, you would not know the difference.

Our object shrinks down to the size of fundamental particles. As the forces approach infinity, the temperature within reaches into the trillions of degrees. The minute black hole does not explode or evaporated because of the intensity of the involved forces. During the latter states of compression the four forces of nature within the object change.

At one level of extreme compression the electromagnetic force unites with the weak force. A much deeper level of compression causes the new electroweak force to unite with the strong force. After more compression, the electroweak/strong force unites with the force of gravity. The theory in physics which explains the unification of all of nature's forces into one new force is the unified field theory (a/k/a the theory of everything). Experiments by tens of thousands of scientists are plodding toward the confirmation of this theory. The cosmological theory of the birth of our universe assumes that the four forces of nature were united before the mother of all explosions occurred billions of years ago.

The unified force fills our object and its immediate environment – including the event horizon. The unified force has replaced all of the other forces. There are now no forces in and around the object other than the unified force. This means that not only have the four forces of nature been assimilated by the new unified force, but also the irresistible applied force and the reaction force have also joined the unified force. The two original forces of our paradox have lost their nature and direction.

For an infinitesimal instant the object exists under the influence of the universal unified force. The universal force flattens or otherwise extends the curvature of the space-time continuum in the immediate environment of the object. There is no gravity. Since the applied force, the reaction force, and gravity are gone, the compression ends. The object expands faster than the speed of light. To keep up with the expanding object, the space-time continuum inflates at a speed that matches the speed of the object's debris. (When the space-time continuum inflates, everything within a defined volume of its space moves faster than the speed of light.)

After the brief moment of inflation, the compression that had united the forces of nature decompressed through the threshold that kept nature's forces together. Through the disintegration of the universal unified force, the four forces of nature regained their integrity. The two forces of our paradox had been assimilated by the universal unified force and changed into the four forces of nature when the object exploded. They have become an indistinguishable part of the forces of the space-time continuum.

The object becomes an expanding globe of gamma rays followed by an expanding hollow sphere of cosmic rays (matter rays). Behind the cosmic rays, the object's plasma spreads in all directions to form an expanding cloud of stable particles and light atoms (such as hydrogen atoms). The paradox of the irresistible applied force against the immovable object has been resolved. The two forces of our paradox and the matter of the object have rejoined our universe.

Having resolved three common paradoxes, we can now proceed with confidence to find the resolution of the creation paradox.

II

The Creation of What Is Real

1. The Interface of the Creator with His Creation

Before the Bible's "In the beginning . . ." God created the world in which spirits live. This supernatural world of spirits is the creator's interface with His creation. To us the supernatural world is known as heaven, hell, paradise, purgatory, the other side, etc. How this supernatural world came to be is described in chapter five. In the fifth chapter a coherent, sensible, and nonmystic description of the Creator, other supernatural beings, and their environment is unveiled along with elaborate quotations from the Bible and the Qur'an.

This chapter describes the creation of the natural world from the point of view of God. The quotations taken from the Bible are broad enough when needed to assure that problems with their contexts are reduced. The quotations from the Qur'an are handled in the same way.

On occasion we will use the term 'life-spirit continuum' when we refer to the supernatural world. (The life-spirit continuum is the medium that enforces the laws that govern the supernatural world in a way that is similar to the enforcement of natural laws by the space-time continuum.)

2. The Creator Makes His Preparations Prior to the
Creation of the Natural World

Creation stories vary from religion to religion. Most are
metaphorical and symbolic. The most clear and most
plausible of these stories is the creation story narrated in
the Bible's book of Genesis. Judaism, Christianity, and
Islam refer to this book to explain the creation and the
Creator.

The description of the creation of our natural world
begins with the Bible's first words.

> In the beginning God created the heaven and
> the earth.
> (Genesis 1: 1 – King James Version [KJV])

This simple sentence masks the complexity of what
happened. The Hebrew scripture of the book of Genesis
used the word shamayim where the King James'
translators wrote 'heaven'. Shamayim is a plural term,
so the King James translators should have written the
plural 'heavens' instead of the singular 'heaven'. With
many heavens the picture of the creation becomes more
complex. Add to this the Hebrew word, Elohim, for God.
This is also a plural term. The plural Elohim could mean
attention to majesty, or it could mean the Godhead of
several divine spirits. Until chapter five, which resolves
the Godhead Paradox, we will observe the creation from
the point of view of the singular Creator.

Our physical heaven (our sky) is a quantitative one.

Its operation is according to natural laws that govern its quantitative cause and effect phenomena. Before the creation of the earth and its natural world, an enforcer of natural laws was needed, so the Creator made the space-time continuum.

The creation of the space-time continuum defined the status of the supernatural world. Since the supernatural world is not governed by quantity bound natural laws, and since natural events cannot occur in the world of spirits, the life-spirit continuum is dimensionless, that is, it has zero dimensions in our world.

The spirit world does use laws that can govern in zero dimensions. These laws are not compatible with natural laws. Because of the incompatibility of the laws of these two continua, the possibility of uniting them into a single efficient system is voided.

A mixture of the two continua would result in chaos. Such chaos would make the creation useless and therefore meaningless. A meaningless creation was averted by the architecture of the Creator's design.

To prevent unintended supernatural happenings from interfering with the processes of the natural world, a barrier exists between the supernatural world and the natural world. (In chapter five we will describe how this barrier functions.) This barrier is supernatural.

When there are communications or transfers from one world to the other, the supernatural barrier converts them into forms that can function within their host continuum.

Except for the Creator and His special agents, no spirit that transfers from the life-spirit continuum to the space-time continuum is permitted to bring supernatural powers with them. The spirits that enter the natural world are converted into nonsupernatural psychic spirits who are subject to natural law. This separation between the supernatural world and the natural world is noted in the Bible and the Qur'an.

> After this manner therefore pray ye: Our Father which art in Heaven, Hallowed be thy name.
> Thy Kingdom come. Thy will be done in earth, as it is in heaven.
> (Matthew 6: 9, 10 – KJV)

> Lay not up for yourselves treasures upon the earth, where moth and rust doth corrupt, and where thieves break through and steal:
> But lay up for yourselves treasures in heaven, where neither moth nor rust doth corrupt, and where thieves do not break through nor steal:
> For where your treasure is, there will your heart be also.
> (Matt 6: 19-21 – KJV)

> He it is Who created
> The heavens and the earth
> In six Days – and His Throne
> Was over the Waters – ...
> (Sura XI: 7 – Abdullah Yusuf Ali Translation [AYAT])

The source of rain was thought by the ancients to come

from above an inverted bowl which held up the 'waters' in the sky. The throne above the waters means that God was beyond physical reach. Although this obsolete view is inadequate today, its meaning is clear: God lives in a world that is different and separate from ours.

Before the creation of the natural world, there was no size, no time, no infinity, and no eternity. From within the life-spirit continuum the Creator reached through the supernatural barrier into the nothingness. With His supernatural powers He created the space-time continuum, infinity, and eternity. This happening created time – a quantifiable measure of processes – and the three dimensions in which events occur. Cause and effect relationships governed by natural laws were established among matter, energy, and forces. The enforcer of natural laws is the space-time continuum. The subjects governed by natural laws are energy, matter, forces, and the intangible medium in the space-time continuum which quantifies events.

When the space-time continuum came into existence, the Creator gave himself an infinite ubiquitous reach and an eternal past. The new conditions of His existence are noted in the Bible and the Qur'an.

> The eternal God is thy refuge, and
> underneath are the everlasting arms: and he
> shall thrust out the enemy from before thee:
> and shall say, Destroy them.
>   (Deuteronomy 33: 27 – KJV)

> For thus saith the high and lofty One that
> inhabiteth eternity, whose name is Holy; I dwell
> in the high and holy place, with him also that is
> of a contrite and humble spirit, to revive the
> spirit of the humble, and to revive the heart of
> the contrite ones.
>   (Isaiah 57: 15 – KJV)

> God! There is no god
> But He, – the Living,
> The Self-subsisting, Eternal.
>   (Sura II: 255 – AYAT)

 Having created the life-spirit continuum, the space-time continuum, infinity, and eternity, the Creator was ready to proceed with the first day of the creation.

3. The Creation During the Earth's First Day

In the beginning the earth was a dust laden, disk-shaped cloud that had two spiral arms and a dense center of mutually orbiting globules of matter. The matter of the earth cloud was a mixture of light elements (such as hydrogen) and the kind of elements found in the debris of supernovas. There were no other objects in the space-time continuum. Since there was no light around or in the earth cloud, the earth was hidden within the darkness of space.

So that His audience of spirits in the life-spirit continuum could observe the creation process, the

Creator used spirit symbol forms and made a visible model earth which was otherwise identical to the physical earth. Because light had not yet been created, all of the features of the earth model were black.

In zero dimensions, that is, in the supernatural world, there is no physical space-time. But the Creator, for the sake of His spirit associates, in a spirit symbol form, made a three dimensional environment that imitated the natural world's cause and effect functions. The Creator synchronized His creation so that what occurred in the space-time continuum also happened in spirit symbol form in the life-spirit continuum. The happenings in both continua are identical, except that the happenings in the life-spirit continuum have a spirit symbol form. In the case of the two earths, what one did, so did the other one. The spirit symbol imitators of real events made everything that happened in the space-time continuum visible to the constituents of the life-spirit continuum. The special value of the spirit symbols of the life-spirit continuum is that they are the spirit symbol essence and existence of whatever existed in the natural world and the supernatural world. Thus, the Creator's audience of spirits learned about the occurrences of the physical earth by watching the spirit symbol earth.

One of the two spiral arms of the model earth cloud was long and the other one was short. The long spiral arm was curved, thick, had tapered edges, and pointed away from the Creator. The short spiral arm was thin, had a slight curve, and pointed at the Creator.

The Creator ordered the earth to rotate. The two earth clouds turned. Each complete revolution was to be counted as one day. As the model earth cloud began its rotation, the short spiral arm turned away from the Creator. The Creator's new timepiece had begun to assign quantities of time (days) to track the steps of His creation process.

While the earth made its slow rotation, the Creator populated the space-time continuum with oceans of water separated by universe sized expanses of space. The number of oceans was infinite. Each ocean was globular shaped because of the gravity of the water. (Most of the gravity was temporarily neutralized to prevent the globular oceans from collapsing into black holes.) For the moment the Creator kept the water of each ocean warm enough to prevent the freezing of the surfaces of these water worlds, but not warm enough to produce light. (Visible light was yet to be created.)

> And the earth was without form, and void;
> and darkness was upon the face of the deep...
> (Genesis 1: 2 – KJV)

Then the Creator sent his Holy Spirit extension throughout the space-time continuum.

> ... and the spirit of God moved upon the face of the waters.
> (Genesis 1: 2 – KJV)

Through the feedback from the ubiquitous Holy Spirit, the Creator guaranteed His omniscience and omnipresence.

As the Creator's agent, the Holy Spirit unleashed the natural force of gravity to convert each ocean into a collapsed universe. The infinite space-time continuum was filled with an infinite number of collapsed universes – each a gargantuan black hole -- which had the potential to be born again. These potential universes were not parallel to each other, within each other, or occupants of more than the three spacial dimensions of the space-time continuum. The space reserved for each of these potential universes was billions of light years across and contiguous with the space reserved for adjacent potential universes.

For each collapsed universe the Creator created an eternal cause and effect past history.

The collapsed universes erupted, and then adapted to their unique histories. The differences among the new universes were unlimited within the boundaries set by natural laws. Most universes had an electromagnetic spectrum which included visible light. Those that did not radiate light had fallen back into being black holes which were too small to give birth to universes that generated visible light.

The histories of most of the visible universes included unending cycles of collapse, expansion, recollapse, and re-expansion. Other histories included the assimilation of parts of other universes, and falling into universes that were on their way to another collapse. Because the measurable age of each universe began again when they exploded into life, and since the beginning of their expansions did not occur at the same moment of their created past, the created ages of the universes varied.

The age of the spiral earth cloud's universe was zero because its content had not yet been released from its black hole. So, even though light had been created, none of it reached the earth from other universes or its own dark unborn universe.

The earth cloud would have remained black if it had been motionless. Because of its rotation and the motion of its matter, the earth produced light when objects collided inside its cloud and when lightning flashed. The two earths had the appearance of a globular disk of sparks that was brightest along its equator.

As stated in the Bible, light had been created.

> And God said, Let there be light: and there was light.
> And God saw the light, that it was good: and God divided the light from the darkness.
> (Genesis 1: 3, 4 – KJV)

Although the earth lacked a sun, a moon, and stars in its sky, the energy from within its cloud of matter produced a dull red glow that could be seen as a background to the brighter flashes of light. Using means which did not violate natural laws, the Holy Spirit organized this dull red glow so that it was brighter on the side that was destined to receive sunlight. Although there was not much difference in the brightness of the two sides, and the lightning and collision flashes could be seen on both sides, this Holy Spirit induced day and night were distinct enough for the audience of spirits to perceive a sunless day side and a moonless night side.

> And God called the light Day, and the
> darkness He called Night. And the evening
> and the morning were the first day.
> (Genesis 1: 5 – KJV)

(Note that because of Hebrew tradition, each day begins at nightfall (the end of the evening) and moves through the next morning into the next evening.)

4. Day two: The Organization of the Waters Above and Below

The short spiral arm of the earth cloud first pointed at the Creator and then turned away from Him to begin the earth's second day.

During the second day the Creator created a cloud of objects, gases, and dust that filled the volume of our present solar system and beyond. This cloud lacked the sun, planets, and moons, but had boulders of ice or frozen gasses, comets, clouds of dust, and clumps of matter (the kinds of matter that are expelled from exploding stars). The diameter of this great cloud was about two light years. This solar system cloud orbited its center volume. This volume of empty space was to be occupied by the sun.

From the solar system cloud, the earth cloud drew matter and grew into a hot planet sized globe. Its molten core of iron and other heavy metals supported a thick layer of magma. The undulating crust was thin, black, and streaked by bright orange and yellow fissures.

Billowing steam rose through torrents of rain that never ceased. Not far above the steam, storm clouds walked over the earth's hot surface with legs of lightning.

Meteors and comets from the solar system cloud streaked through the earth's cloud cover and left trails of whirling particles in their wake. When they collided with the earth's crust, fountains of red, orange, and black magma surged upward through the cloud tops. A few meteors and comets churned through the cloud cover and missed the earth's surface. They returned to space – red with heat if they were asteroids or trailed by ice particles if they were ice comets.

The water from captured boulders of ice and ice comets cooled the earth's surface to a degree that allowed water to cover the crust with a dark worldwide ocean. The rains continued. Steam filled winds drove titanic waves through low storm clouds.

The earth cloud had changed. The spiral arms were gone. Without the spiral arms the earth's rotation was difficult to discern. So the audience of spirits had to be notified when an earth day had passed.

The Bible described what was occurring on the earth.

> And God said, Let there be a firmament in the midst of the waters, and let it divide the waters from the waters.
> And God made the firmament and divided the waters which were under the firmament from the waters which were above the firmament: and it was so.
> And God called the firmament Heaven. And

the evening and the morning were the second
day.
               (Genesis 1: 6-8 – KJV)

5. The Third, Fourth, and Fifth Days: Physical Life Is Created

During the third rotation of the earth, plateaulike land
masses and volcanic islands rose through the earth ocean
into the hot atmosphere. The land masses were overrun
by wide rivers that drained from crater lakes and violent
inland seas.   The rain and lightning continued to be
incessant. Lifted by earthquakes, meteor crashes, and
the bursts of comets, tsunami waves hurled themselves
at the elevated land. Scattered volcanoes had their ash
clouds stripped from their mouths by hurricane force
winds. The earth had responded to the Creator's next
command.

> And God said, Let the waters under the
> heaven be gathered together unto one place,
> and let the dry land appear: and it was so.
> And God called the dry land Earth; and the
> gathering together of the waters called he Seas:
> and God saw that it was good.
>   (Genesis 1: 9, 10 – KJV)

The cloud of matter that had surrounded the earth
disappeared.   The storms became intermittent.   The
atmosphere above the clouds on the day side became blue.
The ocean became dark grey. The plant forerunners of

those that would join in the formation of integrated ecological systems soon covered the land.

> And God said, Let the earth bring forth
> grass, the herb yielding seed, and the fruit tree
> yielding fruit after its kind, whose seed is
> in itself, upon the earth: and it was so.
> And the earth brought forth grass, and herb
> yielding seed after its kind, and the tree
> yielding fruit, whose seed was in itself, after
> his kind: and God saw that it was good.
> And the evening and the morning were the
> third day.
> (Genesis 1: 11-13 – KJV)

The Creator used the growth processes of nature to generate trees and other plants on the earth. Although the processes He used were accelerated, they were nevertheless processes that were similar to those that would be governed by natural laws.

The explosion of our once collapsed universe and the resultant placement of our solar system within our expanding universe were accomplished during the fourth rotation of the earth. Like all of the other universes of the creation, the earth's universe existed within its allocated space.

The Bible describes the Creator's work the fourth day.

> And God said, Let there be lights in the
> firmament of the heaven to divide the day
> from the night; and let them be for signs, and

> for seasons, and for days, and years:
>   And let them be for lights in the firmament
> of the heaven to give light upon the earth:
> and it was so.
>   And God made two great lights; the greater
> light to rule the day, and the lesser light to
> rule the night: he made the stars also.
>   And God set them in the firmament
> of the heaven to give light upon the earth,
>   And to rule over the day and over the night,
> and to divide the light from the darkness:
> and God saw that it was good.
>   And the evening and the morning were
> the forth day.
>   (Genesis 1: 14-19 – KJV)

After the fourth day of the creation of our world, the earth's day and night were determined by the sun's light.

The earth cooled down to the temperatures that were prevalent a few thousand years ago. Ecological systems with marine animals and aviary creatures were created. Their billions of years of cause and effect pasts were created as well. When the Creator created the ancestral past of these new life forms, He installed their fossil records.

The Bible gives an account of this creation process on the fifth day.

> And God said, Let the waters bring forth
> abundantly the moving creature that hath life,
> and fowl that may fly above the earth and in

the open firmament of heaven.

And God created great whales, and every
living creature that moveth, which the waters
brought forth abundantly, after their kind,
and every winged fowl after his kind: and
God saw that it was good.

And God blessed them, saying, Be fruitful,
and multiply and fill the waters in the seas,
and let fowl multiply in the earth.

And the evening and the morning were
the fifth day.

(Genesis 1: 20-23 – KJV)

6. Day Six – Part One: The Creation of Land Animals and the Garden of Eden

During the first part of the sixth day the rest of the animal
kingdom and their ecological systems were created. Their
ancestral fossil records were created to account for the
billions of years of their cause and effect history. Extinct
species of all kinds had their fossil records created to
account for their existence during the created past of the
earth.

The Bible shows this step in the creation process.

And God said, Let the earth bring forth
the living creature after his kind, cattle, and
creeping thing, and beast of the earth after his
kind: and it was so.

And God made the beast of the earth after

> his kind, and cattle after their kind, and
> everything that creepeth upon the earth after
> his kind: and God saw that it was good.
> (Genesis 1: 24, 25 – KJV)

The very important phrase to note in this passage and some of the other passages of the Bible is, "... Let the earth bring forth the living creature..." Here God uses the earth as a tool to bring forth the existence of animals. When something is "brought forth" from something else, the creation is a process. Growth into being is this process. This process is a gathering of water and other earth materials for the formation of living things. The Creator used processes when He created life on earth. On the seventh day of the creation, He assigned the continuation of these processes to the laws of nature.

A few animals were placed in a garden in Eden that would also lodge Adam and Eve. In the life-spirit continuum this garden had an existence in a spirit symbol form. Like their view of the earth model, the audience of spirits could view what transpired in the physical earth's garden by observing its spirit symbol model.

God the Father and the Holy Spirit were the protectors of the garden's constituents.   The area they needed to protect was of limited size. The garden's placement was upon the physical earth's surface. Its substance was physical. The Bible provides the statements needed to come to these conclusions.

> And the Lord God planted a garden
> eastward in Eden;

.   .   .   .

And out of the ground made the Lord God
to grow every tree that is pleasant to the sight,
and good for food, ...

.   .   .   .

And a river went out of Eden to water
the garden; and from thence it was parted,
and became into four heads.
(Genesis 2: 8-10 – KJV)

The garden in Eden's spirit counterpart in the life-spirit
continuum had a spirit symbol form. In the spirit world it
did not need water, sunlight, or gravity. Inside the physical garden on the earth, the Holy Spirit manipulated natural laws to maintain the best of all possible conditions.
Outside the garden, in Eden and elsewhere, natural laws
operated without being manipulated by divinity.

(All universes, ours included, were designed to operate
on their own under the governance of natural laws –
without the need for micromanagement by divinity.)

Even though the garden was being managed by divinity,
it had its own created physical cause and effect history. It
also had its own fossil and geological records.

One of the Holy Spirit's tasks was to use His psychic
powers to provide the garden with an ecology that was
free from noxious plants and animals. In emergency
circumstances, such as lightning, tornados, falling
trees, and meteors, the deflection of these dangers from
creatures in the garden was the responsibility of the
Holy Spirit. This task was not easy because He had to
manipulate natural laws with His psychic powers. The

Creator wanted all routine adjustments in the garden and on the earth to be accomplished through natural law abiding psychic powers.

(Unusual or extreme adjustments to the creation which required supernatural powers were accomplished when the Creator intervened, or when He assigned a supernatural intervention to the Holy Spirit or God the Father.)

The tasks of God the Father in the garden were not the same as those of the Holy Spirit. His role was to be a father and teacher to the garden's anticipated human population. To be effective, He was given the physical body of a male human being while He was in the garden. God the Father talked like a human being, walked like a human being, and cared about air temperature.

> And they heard the voice of the Lord God
> walking in the garden in the cool of the day …
> (Genesis 3: 8 – KJV)

(Remember, like other events in our universe, whatever occurred in the earth bound garden also happened in the garden's counterpart spirit symbol form in the life-spirit continuum.)

7. Day Six – Part Two: the Creation of Adam and Eve

After the land animals were created, Adam and Eve were created from existing materials.

> But there went up a mist from the earth,
> and watered the whole face of the ground.
> And the Lord God formed man of the dust
> of the ground, and breathed into his nostrils the
> breath of life; and man became a living soul.
> (Genesis 2: 6, 7 – KJV)

Water settled upon the ground from the mist before God the Father scooped up dust from the earth. The dust was wet. Adam was made from mud. But this mud contained a multitude of minerals and organic compounds. As is noted in the Qur'an, the quality of the mud was excellent.

> It is He Who has
> Created man from water: ...
> (Sura XXV: 54 – AYAT)

> We created man from sounding clay,
> From mud molded into shape;
> (Sura XV: 26 – AYAT)

(Sounding clay, once hardened, will produce a sound or note when it is tapped.)

This high quality mud was transferred through Adam's body to womankind.

> An the Lord God caused a deep sleep to
> fall upon Adam, and he slept: and he took
> one of his ribs, and closed up the flesh
> instead thereof:

> And the rib, which the Lord God had taken
> from man, made he a woman, and brought
> her unto the man.
>   (Genesis 2: 21, 22 – KJV)

The images of Himself which the Creator gave the first couple were of two kinds: external and internal. His external kind of image included both the male and female human forms. A portion of His internal kind of image was placed within their minds. The Bible explains how this was done.

> And God said, Let us make man in our
> image, after our likeness: and let them have
> dominion over the fish of the sea, and over
> the fowl of the air, and over the cattle, and
> over all the earth, and over every creeping
> thing that creepeth upon the earth.
>   So God created man in his own image, in
> the image of God created he him; male and
> female created he them.
>   (Genesis 1: 26, 27 – KJV)

The Creator is a being that is not flesh. The selection of an anthropomorphic image by the Creator was a practical decision. To be perceived and accepted, whether by human beings or spirits, some kind of embraceable form is needed. Other than its acceptability, our human form is a superficial visible image of little significance to the creation. What has great significance to the creation is the inner image of the Creator. Mankind has a portion of this inner image through a likeness to Him. This partial inner likeness to the Creator provides mankind a means to relate to divinity. This capacity to relate to divinity is expressed in the Qur'an.

> Behold! thy Lord said
> To the angels: "I am about
> To create man, from sounding clay
> From mud molded into shape;
>   "When I have fashioned him
> (In due proportion) and breathed
> Into him of My spirit,
> Fall ye down in obeisance
> Unto him."
>   (Sura XV: 28, 29 – AYAT)

After the creation of Adam and Eve the sixth day of creation ended.

> And God saw every thing that he made,
> and behold, it was very good. And the
> evening and the morning were the sixth day.
>   (Genesis 1: 31 – KJV)

8. The Seventh Day of the Creation

> Thus the heavens and the earth were
> finished and the host of them.
>   And on the seventh day God ended His
> work which he had made; and he rested on
> the seventh day from all his work which he

had made.
>   (Genesis 2: 1, 2 -- KJV)

When the Creator rested, He did nothing more to His creation. Yet, the natural world continued to operate. This means our world has been autonomous since the end of the sixth day of its creation.

Except for rare divine interventions, such as Noah's flood, our world's processes have functioned at a natural rate. The natural laws of gravity and of electromagnetism were the drivers of the flow of water, and the chemistry of plant and animal life.

The Creator used supernatural powers to accelerate the processes governed by the laws of gravity and electromagnetism when He developed the earth. In the quotations that follow, look for the Creator's acceleration of these natural processes.

> And God said, Let the waters under the heaven be gathered together unto one place, and let the dry land appear: and it was so.
> And God called the dry land Earth; and the gathering together of the waters called he Seas: and God saw that it was good.
>   (Genesis 1: 9, 10 – KJV)

> And God said, Let the earth bring fourth grass, the herb yielding seed, and the fruit tree yielding fruit after his kind, whose seed is in itself, upon the earth: and it was so.
> And the earth brought forth grass, and

herb yielding seed after his kind, and the tree
yielding fruit, whose seed was in intself, after
his kind: and God saw that it was good.
(Genesis 1: 11, 12 – KJV)

And God said, Let the earth bring forth the
living creature after his kind, cattle, and
creeping thing, and beast of the earth after
his kind: and it was so.
(Genesis 1: 24 – KJV)

The Bible's "bringing forth" development processes used
forces, matter, and energy to produce universes that
favored the production of intelligent life.

An improvement of a species' ability to survive
enhances the prospect of the production and perpetuation
of intelligent life. The routine mechanisms used by the
Creator are mutation formation and natural selection –
processes He created.

A Relevant Note

We know the Creator can rest, but we also know He has
no need to rest. When the Creator rests, the application
of His will to His creation ceases. We know He applied
His will during the few occasions He did not rest. To rest
is His usual state because of the efficiency of the operation
of His creation. Except for exceptional circumstances, all
supernatural interventions in the natural world ceased
on the seventh day of the creation.

III

The Garden of Eden Anomaly

1. The Special Case of Adam and Eve and the Garden of Eden

Adam and Eve were designed to survive, reproduce, and prevail outside the garden provided they had enough knowledge about shelter, hunting, gathering, child care, and male/female emotional and physical intimacy. Their created past's fossils and archeological records included more than five million years of hominid evolution. If they had been designed to live in the garden forever, they would not have needed the human primate nature that was created for them.

Adam and Eve could have been given a nature that excluded the need to survive, reproduce, control their environment, and promote their self-interest. The garden was a benign environment. Yet, as full grown adults, their bodies were created to function and survive in the indifferent wildernesses of the earth.

In the garden, a ten-year-old was safe, so why did Adam and Eve need to have adult bodies? This circumstance is a suspicious one.

If the garden was meant to be permanent it should have encompassed the earth's surface. But its size was limited to part of Eden on both sides of a section of the Euphrates River. One suspects the garden's limited size and the adult bodies of Adam and Eve meant the garden was a temporary abode for them, and they were scheduled, after they were ready, to enter the earth's inimical wildernesses. The garden's limited size and the specificity of its location are made clear by the Bible.

> And the Lord God planted a garden eastward in Eden; and there he put the man whom he had formed.
> And out of the ground made the Lord God to grow every tree that is pleasant to the sight, and good for food; the tree of life also in the midst of the garden, and the tree of knowledge of good and evil.
> (Genesis 2: 8, 9 – KJV)

The adulthood of Adam and Eve is made clear.

> And they were both naked, the man and his wife, and were not ashamed.
> (Genesis 2: 25 – KJV)

When particular trees, such as the tree of life and the tree of the knowledge of good and evil, were an important part of a garden, the garden had a limited size. To have to walk more than a day to reach important trees was undesirable and unnecessary. A garden managed by divine beings did not need to be large to produce enough food for Adam and Eve, and some of their descendants.

In addition to telling us about the limited size of the garden, the Bible gives us clear reasons to believe the Creator intended for Adam and Eve to leave the garden and enter the wildernesses of the earth.

> So God created man in his own image, in the image of God created he him; male and female created he them.
> And God blessed them, and God said unto them, Be fruitful, and multiply, and replenish the earth, and subdue it: and have dominion over the fish of the sea, and over the fowl of the air, and over every living thing that moveth upon the earth.
> And God said, Behold, I have given you every herb bearing seed, which is upon the face of all the earth, and every tree, in the which is the fruit of a tree yielding seed; to you it shall be for meat.
> And to every beast on the earth, and to every fowl of the air, and to every thing that creepeth upon the earth, wherein there is life, I have given every green herb for meat: and it was so.
> (Genesis 1: 27-30 – KJV)

If Adam and Eve were to remain in the garden forever, there would have been no expectation for them to have dominion over all of the plants and animals of the earth's wildernesses. To gain dominion over nature they had to leave the unnatural garden in Eden and enter the earth's plains, mountains, forests, and jungles. To be successful in accomplishing the expectations of the Creator, and to cope with fatal threats from the earth's plants, creatures, and natural disasters, they needed to be mature and strong.

2. The Status of Adam and Eve in the Garden

Adam and Eve were not the son and daughter of man (mankind). After them many sons and daughters were those of man (mankind). Adam and Eve were the son and daughter of the Creator. The Creator, as progenitor, was their father and mother.

The two adult earthlings never had human parents to nurture, teach, and love them through their development years. So, what they knew about managing their lives and executing their duties in the garden was implanted in their brains by the Creator. Note what the Bible says about Adam (and by default, Eve).

> And the Lord God took the man, and put him into the garden of Eden to dress and keep it.
> (Genesis 2: 15 – KJV)

The ignorance Adam and Eve shared with the other creatures of the earth was about the knowledge of good and evil. This is shown in two statements in the Bible.

> And the Lord God commanded the man,
> saying, Of every tree of the garden thou mayest
> freely eat:
> But of the tree of the knowledge of good
> and evil, thou shalt not eat of it: for in the day
> that thou eatest thereof thou shalt surely die.
> (Genesis 2: 16, 17 – KJV)

> And unto Adam he said, Because thou hast
> hearkened unto the voice of thy wife, and hast
> eaten of the tree, of which I commanded thee,
> saying, Thou shalt not eat of it: cursed is the
> ground for thy sake; in sorrow shalt thou eat of
> it all the days of thy life;
> Thorns also and thistles shall it bring forth
> to thee; and thou shalt eat the herb of the field;
> In the sweat of thy face shalt thou eat bread,
> till thou return unto the ground; for out of it
> wast thou taken: for dust thou art, and unto
> dust shalt thou return.
> (Genesis 3: 17-19 – KJV)

God the Father's proscription against eating the fruit of
the tree of knowledge of good and evil made it clear that
Adam and Eve were not yet mature enough to understand
the contexts for the kinds of behavior that involved good
and evil. Their mentality, then, was that of children, and
would remain so until they could be trained to think like
informed and experienced adults.

Many rules exist for the protection children. For example, a child is told not to walk into a street, or told

not to do what a stranger tells them to do. The violation of either of these rules can result in the death of the child.

Children know that when they are told to obey a rule, its violation is wrong. They did not have to understand the practical and ethical contexts that gave the rule meaning.

Adam and Eve knew that disobedience would not be accepted. Eve showed her understanding of the requirement to obey a rule while she conversed with the talking serpent.

> And the woman said unto the serpent, We
> may eat of the fruit of the trees of the garden:
> But of the fruit of the tree which is in the
> midst of the garden, God hath said, Ye shall not
> eat of it, neither shall ye touch it, lest ye die.
> (Genesis 3: 2, 3 – KJV)

But in our culture a child is not expelled and exiled from her home because she violated a rule and survived. The punishment chosen by God the Father for the rule's violation seems out of proportion with the damage caused. The consequences to Adam and Eve are so extreme one wonders about the character of God the Father. But the consequences of this simple violation reached beyond disobedience and caused irreversible damage to the agenda of the Creator. The decision by God the Father to expel Adam and Eve was forced upon Him. The expulsion from the garden was a practical necessity.

The adult drives of Adam and Eve had been awakened,

but their minds were still immature. They became too distracted to be good apprentices. The garden could no longer be a tool used by the Creator to make progress toward the fulfillment of His agenda. Adam and Eve had to leave the garden and learn to survive in the wilderness by trial and error.

The fulfillment of the Creator's agenda while Adam and Eve resided in the garden would have to be accomplished in the wilderness according to some other program. The garden had become obsolete.

IV

The Creator Creates, Decreates, and Again Creates

1. Divine Creation, Decreation, and Recreation

Not only did the Creator have the capacity to create the past, but also, He was able to recreate the past, and by so doing He could change the cause and effect history of any part of His creation. When He changed the past of an object or being, He recreated the targeted item into a new form (with a new past).

The Qur'an expresses this capacity of the Creator to recreate.

> See they not how God
> Originates creation, then
> Repeats it: truly that
> Is easy for God
>
> Say: "Travel through the earth
> And see how God did
> Originate creation: so will
> God produce a later creation:
> For God has power

Over all things.

. . . ."

(Sura XXIX: 19, 20 – AYAT)

The power to create, decreate, and recreate is the attribute which allowed the Creator to create Darwinian evolution in six days.

The decreation of something is to uncreate its essence and existence by a divine act of annihilation. This divine annihilation returns what exists to a condition of nothingness.

The recreation of something is to subject its essence and existence to a decreation, and then to give it a new essence and existence through a new creation. A recreation is a replacement creation. What had one form and condition is changed into a new form and condition.

When the Creator decreates and recreates something or someone, the decreation and recreation are simultaneous and the passage of time in the space-time zone of action is nihil. This is because the time used was decreated.

As the divine intervention takes place, the past of the subject of the miracle is decreated and recreated to fit the new circumstances. The decreated subject's past has been annihilated and replaced. A decreated past is one that has never occurred.

The essence and existence of the recreated and its replaced past are integrated into the creation and its created past as if they were created in the first six days. The new recreations proceed into the future propelled by their new cause and effect processes, which, along with the rest of the creation, reach back in time into eternity.

Some recreations are limited, and others are unlimited.

From the perspective of a physical observer, an unlimited recreation of her world is one of which she is unaware. This is because her memories of the decreated items have been decreated. The new memories she has of her recreated environment were recreated to be of her changed world. An example of an unlimited recreation is the earth's surface after Noah's flood. (More will be said about the immediate postdiluvian world later in this chapter.)

An example of a limited recreation is the resurrection of Lazarus by Jesus. The observed reversal of irreversible biological processes, and therefore the suspension and violation of natural laws, appears to have taken place. This is because the memories of the witnesses of the miracle were not altered along with the recreation of Lazarus. This miracle came by a decreation of the dead Lazarus and a creation of a living Lazarus. The Bible presents an able Lazarus when he is resurrected.

> Jesus said, Take ye away the stone. Martha, and the sister of him that was dead, saith unto him, Lord, by this time he stinketh: for he hath been dead four days.
>
> Jesus saith unto her, Said I not unto thee, that, if thou wouldest believe, thou shouldest see the glory of God?
>
> Then they took away the stone from the place where the dead was laid. And Jesus lifted up his eyes, and said, Father, I thank

thee that thou has heard me.

And I knew that thou hearest me always:
but because of the people which stand by I said
it, that they may believe that thou hast sent me.

And when he thus had spoken, he cried with
a loud voice, Lazarus, come forth.

And he that was dead came forth, bound
hand and foot with graveclothes: and his face
was bound about with a napkin. Jesus said
unto them, Loose him, and let him go.

Then many of the Jews which came to Mary,
and had seen the things which Jesus did,
believed on him.

(John 11: 39-45 – KJV)

The power to resurrect Lazarus was loaned to the physical Jesus for this particular recreation. Once the resurrection was accomplished, from Jesus, the Creator withdrew this temporary power to recreate the dead. The Creator always takes back any supernatural power He has loaned to a being for a task. This is because the source of all supernatural power is lodged within the Creator in the life-spirit continuum and none other. This isolation of supernatural powers prevents damage, accidental or deliberate, to the two continua of the creation.

When the Creator's purposes are blocked by the operation of natural laws, He violates or suspends the laws by using His supernatural powers. The technique used by the Creator to restore the governance of natural laws after supernatural powers were used is to void or decrease the violations or suspensions that had occurred.

The violations and suspensions of natural laws are decreated and returned to the nothingness. This makes the violations and suspensions fictitious. They never happened – memories or no memories.

Supernatural interventions are rare. We identify supernatural interventions by their violation or suspension of natural law. What is known to be impossible happened, and all credulity is defied.

The Creator uses most of His recreation interventions to adjust the original creation after He has changed His mind, or after He decides that His creation needs to be turned toward a better direction.

2. Notes about Natural Law Abiding Miracles

The preponderance of miracles is not recreations. When recreation is not involved, miracles obey natural laws. Routine miracles are recognized after natural laws have been used and manipulated. The restriction of routine miracles to natural law abiding processes assures the stability of the natural world. The natural law abiding miracles use cause and effect sequences, and maintain precise exchanges of the quantities of matter, energy, and forces. The Creator's agenda is advanced by these miracles without His direct supernatural intervention.

An example of a psychic miracle which used natural laws to accomplish its task is the crossing of the Red Sea by Moses and the twelve tribes of Israel. Every event in the crossing is a natural event.

And it came to pass, when Pharaoh had let
the people go, that God led them not through
the way of the land of the Philistines,
although that was near; for God said,
Lest peradventure the people repent when
they see war, and they return to Egypt:
But God led the people about, through the
way of the wilderness of the Red sea: and the
children of Israel went up harnessed out of the
land of Egypt.
(Exodus 13: 17, 18 – KJV)

And Moses stretched out his hand over the
sea; and the Lord caused the sea to go back by
a strong east wind all that night, and made the
sea dry land, and the waters were divided.
And the children of Israel went into the
midst of the sea upon the dry ground: and the
waters were a wall unto them on their right
hand, and on their left.
(Exodus 14: 21, 22 – KJV)

There are more than twenty words in Hebrew that are
associated with the color red. The word used for red in
the first reference to the Red Sea translates as "reed"
rather than red. So the more accurate translation of
the "Red Sea" is the "Reed Sea". The Sea of Reeds was
located at the northern tip of the Red Sea before the Suez
Canal was constructed, and was considered to be a part
of the Red Sea geology. The waters there were shallow,
affected by tidal drainage, and could be blown aside by

strong winds.

In the time of the Pharaohs, a wilderness was outside the administration of the Egyptian government. The wilderness to which the Israelites trekked was a habitat for wild creatures which was adjacent to the Sea of Reeds, and was an area located southeast of Goshen (the area in the eastern Nile delta occupied by the Hebrew tribes). The regular shores of the Red Sea south of the wilderness area were administered by the Egyptians. The Israelites had no boats, so their common sense choice was to trek from the wilderness across the shallow part of the Sea of Reeds versus crossing a deep part of the sea from shores administered by the Egyptians.

A strong east wind pushed the waters of the Sea of Reeds to the north and to the south. The Israelites crossed the sea at night. Their progress was slow because they had to push against the strong east wind. The intelligent decision of crossing at low tide added to their chances of success.

The events of this miracle were produced by natural law abiding occurrences.

Relevant Notes

The scriptures are replete with natural law abiding miracles. We term these natural law abiding miracles: psychic miracles. We use this term because some minor unexplained events are caused by a natural law abiding mind or by the operators of an unknown technology.

Psychic miracles are events that are untouched by

supernatural influence when they occur, and they happen as a result of one of the Creator's principles. This principle proscribes the suspension and violation of natural laws if other than supernatural means can be used to implement His agenda.

Natural law abiding psychic miracles appear to be supernatural because of our ignorance.

3. The Evident First Recreation: the Serpent of the Garden of Eden

In the garden the serpent could walk with his head high above the ground. He was able to move about without breathing the ground's dust. He did not drag his frame along the ground as snakes do today. The Bible makes this clear.

> And the Lord God said unto the serpent, Because thou hast done this, thou art cursed above all cattle, and above every beast of the field; upon thy belly shalt thou go, and dust shalt thou eat all the days of thy life.
> (Genesis 3: 14 – KJV)

During the serpent's recreation there were three significant thoughts that came to the mind of the Creator. First, the Creator's divine spirit representative, God the Father, was selected as the Creator's divine agent. Second, the Creator no longer wanted an intelligent, skilled in speech, ambulant serpent population roaming the earth. Third, He decided to adjust His creation by recreating the garden's serpent into one which could not calculate, speak, or walk.

The garden's serpent was either a quadruped or bipedal. The Bible does not specify which. The serpent could speak, so, unless he could vocalize like a parrot, his tongue was thick. Either way, he had vocal cords which snakes do not have. The original serpent had a large brain with which to manage abstract verbal symbols (words). Snakes have no such brains. Note the skill with which the serpent used words.

> Now the serpent was more subtil than any beast of the field which the Lord God had made. And he said unto the woman, Yea, hath God said, Ye shall not eat of every tree of the garden?
> And the woman said unto the serpent, We may eat of the fruit of the trees of the garden:
> But of the fruit of the tree which is in the midst of the garden, God hath said, Ye shall not eat of it, neither shall ye touch it, lest ye die.
> And the serpent said unto the woman, Ye shall not surely die:
> For God doth know that in the day ye eat thereof, then your eyes shall be opened, and ye shall be as gods, knowing good and evil.
> (Genesis 3: 1-5 – KJV)

The exchanges of complex abstract thoughts which occurred between the loquacious serpent and the gullible

Eve cannot be managed by the small brain of a snake.

When the Creator recreated the serpent, He also decreated the original serpent's created past. Decreated as well were all of his tracks in the garden and the created fossil records of his ancestors in the ground. The tracks were replaced by the flat imprints of a large snake, and the fossil records of the serpent were replaced by the created fossil records of the ancestors of modern snakes.

The quantities of matter, energy, and forces involved with the essences and existences of the original serpent and the new snakelike serpent were identical. This identity avoided a violation of one of the laws of nature (the law of the conservation of matter and energy).

To Adam and Eve, whose awareness and memories were left intact during the serpent's recreation, the serpent appeared to have elongated as he lost his large head and his appendages. The way they perceived this transformation was passed on from ancestor to descendant through oral tradition.

4. The Evident Second Recreation: the Garden of Eden Is Changed into a Natural Wilderness

The Bible describes the expulsion of Adam and Eve from the garden, and tells us the garden existed on the earth's surface.

Therefore the Lord God sent him forth from the garden of Eden, to till the ground

from whence he was taken.
So he drove out the man; and he placed at
the east of the garden of Eden
Cherubims, and a flaming sword which
turned every way, to keep the way of the tree
of life.
(Genesis 3: 23, 24 – KJV)

Adam and Eve walked into one of the earth's wildernesses
when they were expelled from the garden.

The posting of cherubim also means the garden occupied a small area of the earth. When individual cherubim
are posted to guard one side of the garden, that indicated
the garden was accessible to Adam and Eve on foot.

The garden's existence was dual: on the surface of the
earth and in the supernatural world. The garden existed
in the life-spirit continuum ('heaven') as a spirit symbol
counterpart of the physical garden in Eden.

After the departure of Adam and Eve, the value, meaning, and purpose for the existence of the garden were
voided, so the Creator decreated the earth's only cause
and effect anomaly.

We can be confident this decreation took place
because no trace of the garden in Eden has been found
on the banks of the Euphrates River. Within the space-
time continuum, the decreation of the garden voided
its presence on the earth, annihilated its past history,
and annihilated its geological, fossil, and archeological
records. After this decreation, the garden had never been
created and had never existed (in our world).

Nevertheless, Adam and Eve were witnesses of the

prior existence of the garden because their memories of what they had seen were left intact. The memories of Adam and Eve were real. There had been the garden in Eden. But the absolute decreation of the garden's existence and the decreation of its past converted the status of the memories of Adam and Eve from the recall of real happenings into fiction (in our world).

This is not the case in the life-spirit continuum where the erstwhile existence of the garden, its events, and its created past history are recorded in the form of spirit symbols and spirit images. The history of the garden and its events are preserved in supernatural form.

Relevant Notes

In our world, fictitious thoughts have no quantitative substance or objective verification, and they are mere thought events not aligned with what is real. Like everything else in our world, fictitious thoughts are recorded in spirit symbol form and spirit image form in the life-spirit continuum.

If He wished to decreate what is real, decreate the memories of witnesses, and decreate the spirit symbol records in the life-spirit continuum, the Creator could return what is real into nothingness.

After the garden's decreation, the Creator created a replacement wilderness that was "brought forth" from the vacant acreage the garden had once occupied. The ecology, the past history, the fossil and archeological records, and the geological records of the new wilderness were integrated with those of the surrounding wildernesses.

5. The Worldwide Antediluvian Changes after the Expulsion of Adam and Eve from the Garden

Because of the expulsion of Adam and Eve into the earth's wildernesses and the subsequent recreation of the garden into a replacement wilderness, important adjustments had to be made to the creation by the Creator. A new human race, in addition the Adam and Eve, had to be created. As with everything in the natural world, an eternal cause and effect past which included the creation of new fossil and archeological records had to be created for this new race. Adam and Eve were integrated into this new condition of human existence. The evidence in the Bible for this condition begins with Cain.

> And Cain knew his wife; and she
> conceived, and bare Enoch; . . .
> (Genesis 4: 17 – KJV)

Where did Cain's wife come from? She came from the newly created human race.

There are four reasons why Cain did not marry a sister. First, incest was not necessary since there were available women among the newly created human race. Second, Adam and Eve, being good parents, would not permit any of their daughters to leave their protection to live with a murderer who was likely to kill their daughter. Adam is considered to be the first prophet. If he allowed one of his daughters to leave his protection and allowed her to become a possession of a murderer, then he would have to be characterized as a corrupt prophet. This is not acceptable and was not the case. The first prophet would not abandon one of his children and allow her to become a terrorized target for murder. Third, what sister would want to leave the safety of her home to marry a brother who killed someone she loved (Abel). From where would come the trust and the feeling of security? The fear of infanticide by Cain would increase the fear of an already terrorized woman (if it was Cain's sister). Fourth, Cain was banished from the locale frequented by the family of Adam and Eve. This banishment took place before any sisters were born, so how would Cain ever meet any of his sisters to take them to be his wife? Note how clear the Bible describes the time of the exile of Cain – and more.

> And Cain talked with Abel his brother: and
> it came to pass, when they were in the field,
> that Cain rose up against Abel his brother,
> and slew him.
> And the Lord said unto Cain, Where is Abel
> thy brother? And he said, I know not:
> Am I my brother's keeper?
> And he said, What hast thou done? the
> voice of thy brother's blood crieth unto
> me from the ground.

And now art thou cursed from the earth,
which hath opened her mouth to receive
thy brother's blood from thy hand;
When thou tillest the ground, it shall not
henceforth yield unto thee her strength;
a fugitive and a vagabond shalt thou be in
the earth.
And Cain said unto the Lord, My
punishment is greater than I can bear.
Behold, thou hast driven me out this day
from the face of the earth; and from thy face
shall I be hid; and I shall be a fugitive and a
vagabond in the earth; and it shall come to
pass, that every one that findeth me shall
slay me.
And the Lord said unto him, Therefore
whosoever slayeth Cain, vengeance shall be
taken on him sevenfold. And the Lord set a
mark upon Cain, lest any finding him should
kill him.
And Cain went out from the presence of
the Lord, and dwelt in the land of Nod, on
the east of Eden.
And Cain knew his wife; and she conceived,
and bare Enoch; and he builded a city, and
called the name of the city, after the name of
his son, Enoch.
(Genesis 4: 8-17 – KJV)

From the presence of Adam and Eve, Cain's departure
was immediate. He was exiled east of Eden in the land of

Nod. (Adam and Eve resided in the wilderness of Eden.) Adam and Eve had no other children when Cain departed. Cain and Abel were born at the beginning of their parent's very long lives (long by the Bible's reckoning). The birth of Cain's sisters did not occur until after the birth of the first couple's third son – Seth. That Adam's and Eve's daughters were born during the eight centuries after the birth of Seth meant that they were not available to Cain. The Bible makes this clear.

> And Adam lived an hundred and thirty
> years, and begat a son in his own likeness,
> after his image; and called his name Seth:
> And the days of Adam after he had
> begotten Seth were eight hundred years: and
> he begat sons and daughters:
> And all the days that Adam lived were
> nine hundred and thirty years: and he died.
> (Genesis 5: 3-5 – KJV)

In the land of Nod, Cain found a wife who belonged to a human race the Creator had created before Cain was born.

After the story of Cain's banishment, additional evidence for a created human race is presented in the Bible. When Cain was threatened to be made into a vagabond, his first fear was of being killed by other people he expected to encounter. Being banished from Eden, he was not going to encounter Adam and Eve. And Seth was not yet born. So, for whom are Cain's visible features imprinted with a telling mark? The members of the Creator's new human race were the ones that would be warned to keep their knives, stones, and clubs away from Cain's throat and head.

Cain built a city in the land of Nod and named it Enoch (after his son). A city for whom? His infant son and his wife? The dwellings and shops of the city of Enoch were populated by members of the newly created human race.

6. The Evident Third Recreation: the Postdiluvian World

And God saw that the wickedness of man
was great in the earth, and that every
imagination of the thoughts of his heart was
only evil continually.
     And it repented the Lord that he had made
man on the earth, and it grieved him at
his heart.
     And the Lord said, I will destroy man whom
I have created from the face of the earth;
both man, and beast, and the creeping thing,
and the fowls of the air; for it repenteth me
that I have made them.
     But Noah found grace in the eyes of the Lord.
     (Genesis 6: 5-8 – KJV)

Except for sea faring creatures and corpse eating microbes which could survive in salt water, life on earth was annihilated. So were the ecological systems and their plants. Once the waters were back in their place, the land was contaminated. The lakes, and rivers were brackish and septic. Wherever there had been life, putrid dead animals, corpses, and dead plants littered the ground and waters.

But, ...

> And he stayed yet other seven days; and
> again he sent forth the dove out of the ark;
> And the dove came in to him in the evening;
> and, lo, in her mouth was an olive leaf pluckt
> off: so Noah knew that the waters were abated
> from the earth.
> (Genesis 8: 10, 11 – KJV)

After months of suffocation, cold, and a lack of sunlight under salt water, all of the antediluvian olive trees were dead. The leaf the dove brought back to Noah did not come from one of these dead antediluvian olive trees. Doves are not interested in dead leaves unless they are building a nest. The leaf the dove brought to Noah came from a recreated olive tree that grew within a recreated ecological system on a recreated surface of the earth. All the dead plants, animals, people, and their pasts were recreated into the life on earth that existed about four thousand three hundred years before our time (according to the Bible's chronology). This allowed the people and creatures to leave the ark and resume their routine activities within familiar ecological systems. Without the recreation of the earth's septic surface into one that was vibrant with life, most of the animals and people from the ark would have died. Except for microbes, life on land would have been terminated.

The recreation of the postdiluvian world converted all the dead people, animals, and plants into living plants, animals, and people. Various kinds of active wildernesses were spread over the earth. Created as well were all of the civilizations and tribal organizations of the postdiluvian recreated human race. To obey nature's laws of the conservation of matter and energy, the amounts of energy and matter used in the processes of postdiluvian life were identical to the amounts used by antediluvian life.

The past cause and effect histories of all living things, including those from the ark, were recreated and integrated into the history of the postdiluvian earth. This recreation of the past includes the history of life's genetic development. On the earth, the recreated cause and effect history of genetic development reached back more than a billion years.

The fundamental genetic structures of the postdiluvian human race were adopted from the genetic makeup of Noah's sons. This meant that all human beings shared their fundamental genetic traits with Noah's children. The Bible makes this claim.

> And the sons of Noah, that went forth of the ark, were Shem, and Ham, and Japheth: and Ham is the father of Canaan.
> These are the three sons of Noah: and of them was the whole earth overspread.
> (Genesis 9: 18, 19 -- KJV)

The new genetic features shared by Noah's sons with

the rest of the posdiluvian human race diminished the propensity for violence, but human nature was not altered enough to eliminate evil behavior from among its members.

The billions of years of the earth's recreated past did not include geological records of a worldwide flood in Noah's time. Those records had been decreated except for the memories of the people on the ark. Even though those memories are of real occurrences, since the flood's happenings and their cause and effect pasts were decreated, those happenings never occurred in our world – the space-time continuum. This makes the oral and written records of the witnesses to Noah's flood fictitious in our world.

The geological records of the flood are kept intact in the life-spirit continuum in the form of spirit symbols. In the life-spirit continuum Noah's flood is not fictitious.

The human race that was created in Adam's time ceased to exist after the flood. But this first creation of a human race set the precedent for the second creation of the human race – today's human race. All of today's people have a cause and effect past created for them that reaches back into eternity. The indication of this created past is found in the fossil and archeological records associated with human beings.

The evidence in the Bible for the recreation of the human race after Noah's flood is revealed through the construction of cities by Noah's grandson (Asshur, son of Shem), and Noah's great-grandson (Nimrod, son of Cush and grandson of Ham). Thousands of people were needed to populate these cities. There were more people in these cities than Noah's grandson and great-grandson could reproduce even if they lived as long as the Bible states. The other descendants of Noah were scattered throughout Asia Minor, so they were not contributors to the populations of these cities. The Bible names these two descendants of Noah and the cities they built.

> The children of Shem; Edam, and Asshur,
> and Arphaxad, and Lud, and Aram.
> (Genesis 10: 22 – KJV)

> And the sons of Ham; Cush, and Mizraim,
> and Phut, and Canaan.
> And the sons of Cush; Seba, and Havilah,
> and Sabtah, and Raa-mah, and Sebte-chah:
> and the sons of Raa-mah: Sheba, and Dedan.
> And Cush begat Nimrod: he began to be
> a mighty one in the earth.
> He was a mighty hunter before the Lord:
> wherefore it is said, Even as Nimrod the
> mighty hunter before the Lord.
> And the beginning of his kingdom was Babel,
> and Erech, and Accad, and Calneh, in the land
> of Shinar.
> Out of that land went forth Asshur, and
> builded Nine-veh, and the city Re-hoboth,
> and Calah,
> And Resen between Nine-veh and Calah,
> the same is a great city.
> (Genesis 10: 6 12 – KJV)

In some translations of the Hebrew scripture, Asshur is omitted and Nimrod is credited with the construction of all of the named cities and kingdoms.

Together Asshur and Nimrod built four cities and four kingdoms (or four more cities). The cities and kingdoms had to be populated to justify their status in the Bible. These populations of thousands of people were from the newly created human race. Not mentioned in the Bible are the populations of China, India, Australia, America, the pacific islands, and sub-Saharan Africa.

Relevant Notes

The evolution that was created in six days was restarted on the postdiluvian earth, and continues today. The first creation of evolution took six days to create. The postdiluvian recreation of evolution emerged as the waters receded.

The Creator used the same Darwinian evolution created in the natural world's first six days for the the earth after the flood.

All of the Darwinian evolutionary processes established the first six days continued uninterrupted in the rest of our universe and in all of the creation's other universes.

V

Who or What Is This Creator Who Created Darwinian Evolution in Six Days

1. Before the Bible's "In the beginning . . ."

God created everything. This we know from the Bible's scriptures.

> Who is the image of the invisible God, the
> firstborn of every creature:
> For by him were all things created, that are
> in heaven, and that are in earth,
> visible and invisible, whether they be thrones,
> or dominions, or principalities, or powers:
> all things were created by him, and for him:
> And he is before all things, and by him all
> things consist.
> 　　　(Colossians 1: 15-17 – KJV)

And, . . .

> He hath made the earth by his power,
> he hath established the world by his wisdom,
> and hath stretched out the heaven by his

understanding.

(Jeremiah 51: 15 – KJV)

The Qur'an agrees with these quotations.

He to whom belongs
The dominion of the heavens
And earth: no son
Has He Begotten, nor has He
A partner in His dominion:
It is He Who created
All things, and ordered them
In due proportions.

(Sura XXV: 2 – AYAT)

Since the Creator created everything, He created the beginning of everything. The analysis of His creation will tell us about Him and His agenda. Being good detectives, we will start our investigation at the Bible's, "In the beginning . . ." From there we will have to search backward through a sequence of happenings until we face the divine singularity.

In the book of Genesis the Bible refers to the Creator with His Hebrew name 'Elohim' or 'Elohyim'. Elohim is the plural form of the word Elowahh (God). The Bible validates the view that the plural Elohim was the generic name of the Creator. The consensus interpretation of the plural form of God is that He was being addressed the way kings and magistrates were addressed by others, and when they referred to themselves. But this culturally accepted interpretation cannot exclude the probability that Elohim was a noun which included His spirit, His godliness, His human God the Father component, and His Creator aspect.

Throughout the Old and New Testaments, Elohim chose to manifest Himself to prophets and other sentient beings of His creation through different faces. His faces ranged from the wrathful Jehovah to the phantom Holy Spirit. God is one divine being, but He has chosen to project divine channels of Himself that are distinct identities.

In the book of Genesis, conscious beings encounter three separate divine identities we can investigate. These were the Creator, the Holy Spirit, and God the Father. All three were connected to Elohim.

Christianity settled upon three members of the Godhead: the Holy Spirit, God the Father, and the Son of God. These are three separate spirits. The Godhead is seen as a paradox because the three divine spirits are defined as one Supreme Being. The mathematical expression of this paradox is $1 = 3$, or $3 = 1$.

The New Testament shows an early acceptance of the Godhead vision.

> So, as much as is in me is, I am ready to preach the gospel to you that are at Rome also.
>
> For I am not ashamed of the gospel of Christ: for it is the power of God unto salvation to every one that believeth; to the Jew first, and also to the Greek.
>
> For therein is the righteousness of God revealed from faith to faith: as it is

written, The just shall live by faith.

For the wrath of God is revealed from
heaven against all ungodliness and
unrighteousness of men, who hold the truth
in unrighteousness;

Because that which may be known of God
is manifest in them; for God hath shewed it
unto them.

For the invisible things of him from the
creation of the world are clearly seen,
being understood by the things that are
made, even his eternal power and Godhead;
so that they are without excuse: . . .

(Romans 1: 15-20 – KJV)

Theologians and prophets were mesmerized by the
Godhead concept. They were unable to analyze its parts,
and they were unable to perceive the being represented
by the Godhead symbol.

2. The Functions and Descriptions of the Holy Spirit

Before the creation there was no need for a ubiquitous
presence, so there was none before the beginning, that is,
there was no Holy Spirit. But when God began to create,
the need for the Holy Spirit arose. So the Holy Spirit was
created to be a spirit extension of Himself, and was a part
of the everything He created.

In the Holy Spirit, God had a divine agent that was a
self-aware conscious spirit with a gentle or subtle touch.

With the Holy Spirit, God could avoid the extreme intimidation and panic His divine presence would cause physical beings. The Holy Spirit is God's divine resident agent in the churches, organizations, and individuals who are willing to interact with Him. It is through the Holy Spirit that the preponderance of God's communication with other beings takes place. The Bible gives us insights into the nature and functions of the Holy Spirit.

> But God hath revealed them unto us by his spirit: for the Spirit searcheth all things, yea, the deep things of God.
> For what man knoweth the things of a man, save the spirit of man which is in him? even so the things of God knoweth no man, but the Spirit of God.
> Now we have received, not the spirit of the world, but the spirit which is of God; that we might know the things that are freely given to us of God.
> Which things also we speak, not in the words which man's wisdom teacheth, but which the Holy Ghost teacheth, comparing spiritual things with spiritual.
> (1 Corinthians 2: 10-13 – KJV)

In the Old Testament God's spirit is mentioned early in the book of Genesis.

> And the earth was without form, and void; and darkness was up on the face of the deep.

> And the Spirit of God moved upon the face
> of the waters.
> > (Genesis 1: 2 – KJV)

The Holy Spirit spoke to prophets.

> For the prophesy came not in old time by
> the will of man: but holy men of God spoke
> as they were moved by the Holy Ghost.
> > (II Peter 1: 21 – KJV)

The Qur'an interprets the Holy Spirit of the Creator with less emphasis, and "Holy Spirit" is not capitalized.

> Those apostles
> We endowed with gifts,
> Some above others:
> To one of them God spoke;
> Others He raised
> To degrees (of honour);
> To Jesus the son of Mary
> We gave Clear (Signs),
> And strengthened him
> With the holy spirit.
> > (Sura II: 253 – AYAT)

Having an independent identity and consciousness and a light touch, the Holy Spirit is the best medium for the awareness, transfer, and answer to prayers. On routine matters the Holy Spirit will communicate directly with those praying.

3. The Functions and Descriptions of God the Father

Another divine spirit extension of God that was a part of everything He created was God the Father. Before the creation there was God, but there was no God the Father.

After the creation, God the Father often confronted the Hebrews when He wore His Jehovan face. During those confrontations He was a divine spirit extension of God -- not the Creator Himself. God the Father was created to manage specific tasks God assigned to Him. God the Father's physical presence in the garden in Eden is an example of His execution of one of the tasks given to Him by God.

In His spirit and physical form, God the Father has human nature. He is an independent, autonomous, self-aware conscious divine spirit being who has His own identity. Like a changeling, He has a multitude of faces and adapts His appearance to manage conditions which challenge Him.

In the Old Testament God the Father was the task master: Jehovah. When God the Father was Jehovah He functioned the way controlling and authoritarian human beings functioned when they ruled people and territory. (God did not entrust God the Father with unlimited supernatural powers because He had human nature, and God does not entrust beings who have human nature with unlimited supernatural powers.)

God the Father is an interactive divinity. Within limits, He had permission from God to function as He wished. He acted as an independent contractor for God. Only His assignments, his own character, and God kept His human nature under control. God the Father, a/k/a Jehovah, expresses love, anger, frustration, fear, and a tendency to destroy when His fury overcame his patience. He is not an evil god, but the Old Testament is a record of a multitude of evil acts He committed because of His human nature.

In the Bible we see Jehovah when He interacts with Moses, and when He expresses His fury at the Israelites.

> And the Lord said unto Moses, Go get thee down; for thy people, which thou broughtest out of the land of Egypt, have corrupted themselves:
> They have turned aside quickly out of the way which I commanded them: they have made them a molten calf, and have worshipped it, and have sacrificed thereunto, and said, These be thy gods, O Israel, which have brought thee up out of the land of Egypt.
> And the Lord said unto Moses, I have seen this people, and behold, it is a stiffnecked people:
> Now therefore let me alone, that my wrath may wax hot against them, and that I may consume them: and I will make thee a great nation.
> (Exodus 32: 7-10 – KJV)

Here Jehovah is angry enough to exterminate the Israelites and start over with Moses (with an altogether different people).

But God the Father, Jehovah, changes His mind and again shows His warm human side.

> And Moses besought the Lord his God, and said, Lord, why doth thy wrath wax hot against thy people, which thou hast brought forth out of the land of Egypt with great power, and with a mighty hand?
>
> Wherefore should the Egyptians speak, and say, For mischief did he bring them out, to slay them in the mountains, and to consume them from the face of the earth? Turn from thy fierce wrath, and repent of this evil against thy people.
>
> Remember Abraham, Isaac, and Israel, thy servants, to whom thou swarest by thine own self, and saidist unto them, I will multiply your seed as the stars of heaven, and all this land that I have spoken of will I give unto your seed, and they shall inherit it for ever.
>
> And the Lord repented of the evil which he thought to do unto his people.
>   (Exodus 32: 11-14 – KJV)

Allah, the god of Islam, and Jehovah are the same divinity, as is shown by these passages from the Qur'an.

> We took the Children of Israel

(With Safety) across the sea.
They came upon a people
Devoted entirely to some idols
They had. They said:
"O Moses! fashion for us
A god like unto the gods
They have." He said:
"Surely ye are a people
Without Knowledge.

"As to these folk, --
The cult they are in
Is (but) a fragment of a ruin,
And vain is the (worship)
Which they practice."

He said: Shall I seek for you
A god other than the (true)
God, when it is God
Who hath endowed you
With gifts above all nations?"

And remember We rescued you
From Pharaoh's people,
Who afflicted you with
The worst penalties,
Who slew your male children
And saved alive your females:
In that was a momentous
Trial from your Lord.
      (Sura VII: 138-141 -- AYAT)

> But those will prosper
> Who purify themselves,
>
> And glorify the name
> Of their Guardian – Lord
> And (lift their hearts)
> In Prayer.
>
> Nay (behold), ye prefer
> The life of this world;
>
> But the Hereafter
> Is better and more enduring.
>
> And this is
> In the books
> Of the earliest (Revelations), --
> The Books of
> Abraham and Moses.
>   (Sura LXXXVII: 14-19 – AYAT)

Jehovah shows the dark side of His human nature again: extreme intolerance. This is an intolerance born out of fear. He advocates murder of nonbelievers. This trait of Jehovah is straight out of His human nature.

> And that prophet, or that dreamer of
> dreams, shall be put to death; because he hath
> spoken to turn you away from the Lord your
> God, which brought you out of the land of
> Egypt, and redeemed you out of the house of

bondage, to thrust thee out of the way which the Lord thy God commanded thee to walk in. So shalt thou put the evil away from the midst of thee.

If thy brother, the son of thy mother, or thy son, or thy daughter, or the wife of thy bosom, or thy friend, which is as thine own soul, entice thee secretly, saying,
Let us go and serve other gods, which thou hast not known, thou, nor thy fathers;

Namely, of the gods of the people which are round about you, nigh unto thee, or far off from thee, from the one end of the earth even unto the other end of the earth;

Thou shalt not consent unto him, nor harken unto him; neither shall thine eye pity him, neither shalt thou spare, neither shalt thou conceal him:

But thou shalt surely kill him; thine hand shall be first upon him to put him to death, and afterwards the hand of all the people.

And thou shall stone him with stones, that he die; because he hath sought to thrust thee away from the Lord thy God, which brought thee out of the land of Egypt, from the house of bondage.
(Deuteronomy 13: 5-10 – KJV)

The Qur'an agrees with this attitude of Jehovah.

Why should ye be

Divided into two parties
About the Hypocrites?
God hath upset them
For their (evil) deeds.
Would ye guide those
Whom God hath thrown
Out of the Way? For those
Whom God hath thrown
Out of the Way, never
Shalt thou find the Way.

They but wish that ye
Should reject Faith,
As they do, and thus be
On the same footing (as they):
But take not friends
From their ranks
Until they flee
In the way of God
(From what is forbidden).
But if they turn renegades,
Seize them and slay them
Wherever ye find them;
And (in any case) take
No friends or helpers
From their ranks; --
    (Sura IV: 88, 89 – AYAT)

Then, according to the Qur'an, Allah (Jehovah) is again merciful.

> "And ordain for us
> That which is good,
> In this life
> And in the Hereafter:
> For we have turned unto Thee."
> He said: "With My Punishment
> I visit whom I will;
> But My Mercy extendeth
> To all things. That (Mercy)
> I shall ordain for those
> Who do right, and practise
> Regular charity, and those
> Who believe in Our Signs; --
> (Sura VII: 156 – AYAT)

Another time His wrath returns, as is shown in the Qur'an.

> Did the people of the towns
> Feel secure against the coming
> Of Our Wrath by night
> While they were asleep?
> (Sura VII: 97 – AYAT)

The certainty that Jehovah has human nature is shown in the Scriptures when He permits the dark side of His human nature to persuade Himself to order genocide. The first phase of this genocide was committed against the people of Jericho. When this town was captured by the Israelites, all of the inhabitants were slaughtered according to Jehovah's command – even the male and female children, babies, and infants.

> Now Jericho was straitly shut up because of
> the children of Israel: none went out, and
> none came in.
>
> .   .   .   .
> So the people shouted when the priests
> blew with the trumpets: and it came to pass,
> when the people heard the sound of the
> trumpet, and the people shouted with a great
> shout, that the wall fell down flat, so that the
> people went up into the city, every man straight
> before him, and they took the city.
> And they utterly destroyed all that was in the
> city, both man and woman, young and old, and
> ox, and sheep, and ass, with the edge of the
> sword.
>
> .   .   .   .
> And they burnt the city with fire, and all
> that was therein: only the silver, and the gold,
> and the vessels of brass and of iron, they put
> into the treasury of the house of the Lord.
> And Joshua saved Rehab the harlot alive,
> and her father's household, and all that she
> had; and she dwelleth in Israel even unto this
> day; because she hid the messengers, which
> Joshua sent to spy out Jericho.
> (Joshua 6: 1, 20, 21, 24, 25 -- KJV)

The saving of Rehab and her relatives was not an
act of mercy. It was a reward for providing valuable

assistance. As most human beings would have done, Jehovah allowed this exception.

The Scriptures showed the effective and efficient execution of the genocide of the population of one conquered town after another.

> And it came to pass, when Israel had made an end of slaying all the inhabitants of Ai in the field, in the wilderness wherein they chased them, and when they were all fallen on the edge of the sword, until they were consumed, that all the Israelites returned unto Ai, and smote it with the edge of the sword.
> And so it was, that all that fell that day, both men and women, were twelve thousand, even all the men of Ai.
> For Joshua drew not his hand back, wherewith he stretched out the spear, until he had utterly destroyed all the inhabitants of Ai.
> (Joshua 8: 24-26 – KJV)

> And that day Joshua took Makkedah, and smote it with the edge of the sword, and the king thereof he utterly destroyed, them, and all the souls that were therein; he let none remain: and he did to the king of Makkedah as he did unto the king of Jericho.
> (Joshua 10: 28 – KJV)

Joshua next captured and slaughtered the inhabitants

of Libnah, Lachish, Gezer, Eglon, Hebron, Debir, and
Hazor. (These towns are listed in the Bible as part of the
killing fields of the advancing Hebrews.)

This first phase of the Israelite conquest of their
promised land is summarized in one of the verses of the
Bible.

> So Joshua smote all the country of the hills,
> and of the south, and of the vale, and of the
> springs, and all their kings: he left none
> remaining, but utterly destroyed all that
> breathed, as the Lord God of Israel commanded.
> (Joshua 10: 40   KJV)

Jehovah, not Moses, ordered the genocide when the Israelites invaded their promised land.

> As the Lord commanded Moses his servant,
> so did Moses command Joshua, and so did
> Joshua; he left nothing undone of all that the
> Lord commanded Moses.
> (Joshua 11: 15 – KJV)

Jehovah showed his human nature again when He adopted a near nihilistic fury before Noah's flood.

> And, behold, I, even I, do bring a flood of
> waters upon the earth, to destroy all flesh,
> wherein is the breath of life, from under
> heaven; and every thing that is in the earth
> shall die.

(Genesis 6: 17 – KJV)

The Creator let Jehovah have His way for the destruction of the first human race, but He had to repair Jehovah's damage with a recreation after the flood. Destructive power was taken away from Jehovah by the Creator, and this interpretation is supported by the limits to Jehovah's powers that show He is not an ultimate omnipotent divine being.

Why did Jehovah have human nature? The answer is simple. The Israelites were an obstinate, "stiffnecked" people. Few of them would have followed a god out of Egypt who had the character of Jesus. The Israelites would not have followed a Jesuslike god for forty years in the wilderness. The Israelites wanted a divinity that would order a genocide. The Hebrews had to have a deity with a human nature and character that was tougher and more cruel than the leaders of their adversaries – including the pharaoh.

4. Descriptions of the Creator

When we peer into the supernatural world to see God, we perceive the Creator. Prophets have provided some glimpses of the supernatural world, so we will use these visions to describe the Creator.

Ezekiel tells us about the substance of His throne.

> And above the firmament that was over
> their heads was the likeness of a throne, as the
> appearance of a sapphire stone: . . .

(Ezekiel 1: 26 – KJV)

The Qur'an tells us where the throne is located.

> He it is Who created
> The heavens and the earth
> In six Days – and His Throne
> Was over the Waters – . . .
> (Sura XI: 7 – AYAT)

The waters in this case are the waters above the firmament. The firmament was what the ancient cosmologists believed was an upside-down bowl and its inner volume which formed the sky's dome over the earth. The firmament supported a layer of water lodged on the exterior of the bowl. These waters were the ancient's explanations for the source of rain water. The throne mentioned in the Qur'an was located over the layer of waters above the firmament.

In the Old Testament, Daniel gives us a distinct vision of the Creator in his supernatural dwelling.

> Then I lifted up mine eyes, and looked, and behold a certain man clothed in linen, whose loins were girded with fine gold of Uphaz:
> His body also was like beryl, and his face as the appearance of lightning, and his eyes as lamps of fire, and his arms and his feet like in colour to polished brass, and the voice of his words like the voice of a multitude.
> (Daniel 10: 5, 6 – KJV)

In a vision similar to Daniel's, John tells us he saw the Creator and the throne. (Most of the descriptions of the happenings in the life-spirit continuum are found in the New Testament's book of The Revelation of John.)

> And immediately I was in the spirit: and behold, a throne was set in heaven, and one sat on the throne.
> And he that sat was to look upon like a jasper and sardine stone: and there was a rainbow round about the throne, in sight like unto an emerald.
> And round about the throne were four and twenty seats: and upon the seats I saw four and twenty elders sitting, clothed in white raiment; and they had on their heads crowns of gold.
> And out of the throne proceeded lightnings and thunderings and voices: and there were seven lamps of fire burning before the throne, which are the seven spirits of God.
> And before the throne there was a sea of glass like unto crystal: . . .
> (Revelation 4: 2-6 – KJV)

That the life-spirit continuum had a floor is evidence that God gave His created spirits an environment with the appearance of the natural world. This tells us that spirits needed to orient themselves the way we do. For example, the glass floor is situated between up and down. Yet, in the zero dimensions of the life-spirit continuum, there is no up and down. The appearance of up and down, not their actuality, was installed by God for the sake of the perceptions of conscious spirit beings.

The Creator, standing near the throne, is described by John.

> And in the midst of the seven candlesticks one like unto the Son of man, clothed with a garment down to the foot, and girt about the paps with a golden girdle.
> His head and his hairs were white like wool, as white as snow; and his eyes were as a flame of fire.
> And his feet like unto fine brass, as if they burned in a furnace; and his voice as the sound of many waters.
> And he had in his right hand seven stars: and out of his mouth went a sharp twoedged sword: and his countenance was as the sun shineth in his strength.
> (Revelation 1: 13-16 – KJV)

Behind the glitter of this vision is the Creator Divine Spirit of Essence and Existence. In our world He created both our essence and our existence. He created the essence and existence of everything else in our world as well.

To find the essence and existence of God, we leave the natural world behind us and we dive into the supernatural world – the life-spirit continuum.

When we move into the life-spirit continuum we enter a world that has zero dimensions with respect to the space-time continuum. In zero dimensions there is no space-time continuum, no energy, no matter, no virtual particles, no virtual energy, no forces, no cause and effect occurrences and their interactions, and no natural laws. The laws of the life-spirit continuum apply only to its constituents. These constituents are all made of spirit.

As described in the Bible, the supernatural world (the life-spirit continuum and its spirit beings) is ephemeral, fanciful, dreamlike, and not amenable to our perceptions. This strange environment seems to operate according to cause and effect processes like those in our world, but this is an illusion established by God for the sake of the perceptions of the constituents of the life-spirit continuum. A world that seems to function like the natural world allows the spirit beings to relate to each other and to their environment. The happenings in the supernatural world do happen, but they do not happen as one perceives them to happen. They happen in a way that is different from the way occurrences take place in the natural world. The main difference is that there are no systematic cause and effect relationships in the supernatural world.

Spirit beings, spirit symbol entities, and spirit deities are the created constituents of the supernatural world. The Creator is one of these divine spirits. His commission by God was to create everything that was not made of spirit -- the natural world.

The Creator in the book of Genesis is not a transformation of God into a divine spirit creator. The Creator is the created spirit representation of God. The Creator is a member of the Godhead. (The Godhead hides God from us.)

To reach God behind the Godhead, and to resolve the Godhead paradox, the components of the Godhead must be seen in a monotheistic context. Monotheists can agree there was but one Creator, so He is where we will begin our examination.

The home of the Creator is the supernatural world (the life-spirit continuum). In the life-spirit continuum the constituents are made of spirit. Some of these spirits are conscious and others are not. Spirits, the divine kind and the nondivine kind, are imperishable. An example of a nondivine conscious spirit is the cherub, Lucifer.

> Thou art the anointed cherub that covereth;
> and I have set thee so: thou wast upon the holy
> mountain of God: thou hast walked up and
> down in the midst of the stones of fire.
> (Ezekiel 28: 14 – KJV)

(The stones of fire are interesting, and they are probably related to the creative action of the Creator. It is evident that their distribution is such that spirits are able to walk among them.)

The Creator is a divine spirit, like God the Father and the Holy Spirit.

> God is a spirit: and they that worship him
> must worship him in spirit and in truth.
> (John 4: 24 – KJV)

His divinity is in addition to this spirit component. The spirit component of the Creator is the same as Lucifer, the stones of fire, angels, spirit symbols, and the life-spirit continuum. To all that exists in the supernatural world, there is this commonality of spirit. Being made of spirit is a common feature. A uniqueness of kind does not exist among beings and things made of spirit.

Because He is made of spirit, the Creator is not unique in an absolute way. Nor is He unique in His divinity. Also divine are the Holy Spirit, God the Father, and the Godhead.

We must look through the commonality of the Creator to find the uniqueness of God. We know from the Bible and the Qur'an that God is unique.

The Qur'an looks through the Creator and reports its findings.

> No vision can grasp Him,
> But His grasp is over
> All vision: He is
> Above all comprehension,
> Yet is acquainted with all things.
> (Sura VI: 103 – AYAT)

The Bible uses a unique name for the unique being be-hind the Godhead.

> In the beginning was the Word, and the
> Word was with God, and the Word was God.
> The same was in the beginning with God.
> All things were made by him; and without
> him was not any thing made that was made.
> In him was life; and the life was the light

of men.

And the light shineth in darkness; and the darkness comprehended it not.

There was a man sent from God, whose name was John.

The same came for a witness, to bear witness of the Light, that all men through him might believe.

He was not that Light, but was sent to bear witness of that Light.

That was the true Light, which lighteth every man that cometh into the world.

He was in the world, and the world was made by him, and the world knew him not.

.   .   .   .

And the Word was made flesh, and dwelt among us, (and we beheld his glory, the glory as of the only begotten of the Father,) full of grace and truth.

.   .   .   .

And of his fullness have all we received, and grace for grace.

For the law was given by Moses, but grace and truth came by Jesus Christ.

No man hath seen God at any time; the only begotten Son, which is in the bosom of the Father, he hath declared him.

(John 1: 1-10, 14, 16-18 – KJV)

From the Christian perspective, when we look through the divine spirit of the Creator, we are looking through

Jesus. In the life-spirit continuum, Jesus is a spirit extension of the Word. The Word is the being behind the Godhead. The Word is God.

Again, from the Christian perspective, the Word was the being who used a Creator divine spirit extension during creations, decreations, and recreations. Then, in the time of Jesus, the Word created His Jesus divine spirit extension, and then created His Jesus material representation on earth. The chain of connection after the creation of Jesus was, beginning with the Word: the Word, His created spirit (who could act as either the Creator spirit or as the Jesus spirit), and the material (human) Jesus.

Continuing along the Christian perspective, the divine spirits of the Creator and Jesus are the same spirit. After the death of the physical Jesus, the Son of God title was given to the Creator divine spirit by Christians. In the Godhead ensemble, Jesus the Son of God is the face of the Creator spirit. Their minds are the same, and the mind of the being behind the Godhead, God Himself, is the same as these two spirits. If we look through Jesus the Son of God divine spirit we are channeled through the Creator to the Word.

The Word, even when He speaks as the Creator to Isaiah, does not have human nature.

> For my thoughts are not your thoughts,
> neither are your ways my ways, saith the Lord.
> For as the heavens are higher than the earth,
> so are my ways higher than your ways, and
> my thoughts than your thoughts.

(Isaiah 55: 8,9 -- KJV)

5. The Ultimate Creator

For a while we will use the title "Ultimate Creator" in the place of the "Word", because the "Word" is an exclusive Christian name.   "Ultimate Creator" can be anyone's name for the Supreme Being.

The Ultimate Creator created His Godhead spirit ensemble to interface with His creation. The Ultimate Creator created the supernatural barrier, the life-spirit continuum, the creation's spirit components and constituents, and the divine spirit group known as the Godhead. The Creator divine spirit member of the Godhead, a/k/a God, is a direct spirit representation of the Ultimate Creator. The Ultimate Creator's consciousness is extended from Him through God to His creation. God the Father and the Holy Spirit are indirect extensions of the Ultimate Creator.

The Godhead is made of divine spirit. The Ultimate Creator is not made of any kind of spirit. He is nonmaterial in a way that is not of spirit. Yet He has found a way to touch us through His divine spirit representatives. Through the action of His direct spirit representative, the Creator, a/k/a God, He has found a way to put a potential likeness to Himself in human beings without creating an imitation of Himself or making a replica of Himself. There are no imitations or replications of Him in His creation either. Everything which He created is other than an imitation or replication of Himself.

That nothing in the life-spirit continuum and the space-time continuum is a reproduction of His constitution makes Him unique in an absolute way – a singularity.

Some items in the creation are unique, but they are unique in a relative way. Their uniqueness is relative because some of their aspects are in common with other items of the creation. They vary from these aspects in amount and quality. Each bright star varies in the number of electrons they contain, but this uniqueness is relative because they have electrons in common. Angels and demons have unique features, but they are unique in a relative way because their configurations are variations of spirit.

The Bible and the Qur'an tell us that God is unique, and the uniqueness they mean is one that is absolute.

The Qur'an is clear about this.

> Say: He is God,
> The One and Only:
>
> God, the Eternal, Absolute;
>
> He begetteth not,
> Nor is He begotten;
>
> And there is none
> Like unto Him.
>   (Sura CXII: 1-4 – AYAT)

And the Bible says:

> Remember the former things of old: for I
> am God, and there is none else; I am God,
> and there is none like me,
> (Isaiah 46: 9 – KJV)

These statements tell us there is only one God and there is nothing like Him. This is an absolute kind of uniqueness.

An absolute uniqueness is one which has nothing in common with anything else. The excepted elements that are shared are existence, divinity, and consciousness. Otherwise you will find nothing in God's essence which has anything in common with the essence of anything else.

An essence that has an absolute uniqueness cannot be reproduced, recreated, replicated, or multiplied. An absolute uniqueness proscribes the creation of any other entity that has anything in common with Him. Such a creation would void His absolute uniqueness.

The Godhead has three beings who share a spirit constitution. This spirit feature of the members of the Godhead is divine, but the Godhead entities share the same spirit element used to configure angels and demons. Angels, demons, and the members of the Godhead are unique in a relative way. All beings in the life-spirit continuum are unique in a relative way, so none qualify as the Ultimate Creator singularity.

For the Ultimate Creator to have an absolute uniqueness requires His constitution to be made of elements that are other than the elements that exist in the life-spirit continuum and the space-time continuum.

The Ultimate Creator is made neither of matter, nor of energy, nor of forces, nor of the space-time fabric, nor of any part of a continuum, nor of any kind of spirit.

6. The Existential Condition of the Ultimate Creator

Nothingness and the Ultimate Creator were in a state of union before the creation of everything. The Ultimate Creator was within the nothingness and from the nothingness was not separate.

The nothingness was an absolute void. It was the opposite of everything. In the nothingness there were no spirits, no continua, no dimensions, no natural laws, no supernatural laws, no other laws, no constituents, no time, no place, no value, no meaning, and no purpose.

From our human perspective, the nothingness is a state that is not the same as what is nothing. If you have nothing in front of you and placed an object therein, you would have in front of you an object and nothing. If you did the same with the nothingness in front of you, the object would change from being something to being nothing. The nothingness would void the existence of the object. If you jumped into the nothingness, your body would disappear, your soul would cease, and your spirit would turn into nothingness. For you, there would be no more memories or thoughts, and certainly no afterlife.

Existence and essence do not happen in the nothing-ness, and if these entered the placeless nothingness, they would be voided. Whatever was a placeless presence within the nothingness was equal to being nothing. This is true of omniscience, omnipotence, and consciousness.

Within the nothingness, the state of being of the Ultimate Creator was concomitant with being nothing. Because the nothingness was placeless, there could be no omnipresence. Because everything was yet to be created, nothing could be known, so there could be no omniscience. Since there were no continua and their constituents in the nothingness, there could be no omnipotence. Omnipresence, omniscience, and omnipotence had potential, but they were not actual states.

The Ultimate Creator's cognitive consciousness was confined to be about nothing or to be about what was a potential to be everything. He had awareness and was aware that his state of being was insignificant. Significance would have to be created before He could have significance.

When the Ultimate Creator thought about His external environment, He thought about nothing. When He focused upon His internal environment He thought about nothing, unless, within his imagination, He created a fantasy of what He would prefer to be and how He preferred to be.

Before the creation of anything, the Ultimate Creator's fantasies covered the infinite number of alternative styles of essence and existence for Himself and for the creation of His external environment. He elected to create an external environment that would fulfill His search for value, meaning, and purpose – and significance. The Ultimate Creator's creation was to be the best possible everything He could create to fulfill His agenda. He found that to achieve His agenda,

He needed a supernatural world and a natural world.

The Ultimate Creator created the supernatural world first. All of the entities of the supernatural world are made of spirit symbols. Spirit symbols are the essence and existence of what they symbolize. The laws that govern them are the laws that govern symbol spirits. (These laws have counterparts in the laws that govern symbols in our world.) The spirits of the supernatural world are fixed in their configurations, and they are absolute in their essence. Because of this, the supernatural world is nondevelopmental. It is not in the supernatural world the Ultimate Creator would find the fulfillment of His agenda – an agenda that necessitates development.

When the Ultimate Creator, through the Creator divine spirit, created the quantitative natural world, He made it developmental. The quantities and laws of the natural world were designed by Him to generate intelligent self-aware physical beings who would have the likenesses to Him which He selected. A developmental natural world was flexible enough, and had enough variety to find pathways that could compete with the natural world's convergent determinism. Development in the natural world was divergent. This divergence interplayed with deterministic quantities and laws to produce a multitude of possibilities. Once intelligent self-aware physical beings evolved, they could choose their destinies from a broad list of options. This allowed the existence of free wills. Once free wills were established, physical beings could pursue the acquisition of a number of available likenesses to the Ultimate Creator. The Ultimate Creator could identify with physical beings who had acquired some of these likenesses. This kind of achievement by autonomous physical beings terminated His isolation.

To the Ultimate Creator, the supernatural world is an instrument He uses to relate to the rest of His creation. The value, meaning, and purpose of an instrument is in its use and usefulness, but the user of the instrument does not find value, meaning, and purpose for himself within the instrument. The Ultimate Creator uses the members of the Godhead and the rest of the life-spirit continuum as a tool to fulfill His agenda – to find value, meaning, and purpose for Himself.

7. The Rebellion of the Ultimate Creator

As previously stated, before anything was created the status quo for the Ultimate Creator was to be concomitant with the nothingness. This we know: He rejected and took action against the status quo by creating everything. The Ultimate Creator rebelled against His association with the nothingness. He rejected being potential, and otherwise being nothing. To separate Himself from the nothingness, He knew He had to be active.

(This is a definite rebellion by the Ultimate Creator, because rebellion is the taking of action against a status quo after the status quo has been rejected.)

The Ultimate Creator insulated Himself from the nothingness by creating a supernatural barrier that enveloped Him and simultaneously created the life-spirit continuum which provided Him with an external environment. Both the continuum and the barrier were made of spirit.

Yet, He is not made of spirit. We cannot know of what He is made. He was made of something. We have referred to Him as the Ultimate Creator, but henceforth we will identify Him as the Somethingness.

There is but one unit of this nonspirit divinity. There is nothing in everything that is like Him. Since He is not made of spirit, He cannot be a part of the Godhead of divine spirits, even though His consciousness is extended into the God (Creator) member of the Godhead.

8. The Resolution of the Godhead Paradox

The monotheistic insistence that the Godhead is one divinity which has three separate divine spirit entities forces the acceptance of the "one is three" paradox. The paradox persisted because any being beyond the Godhead was perceived as another divine spirit.

Had the Somethingness been a divine spirit there would be a perpetual Godhead paradox. Since the divine singularity is the Somethingness, and the Somethingness is not a spirit, He is a distinct and separate entity, and is not a spirit part of the Godhead. The Godhead is there-fore three divine spirit beings and is not united into any kind of single divine spirit. Each member of the Godhead is a divine spirit instrument (interface with the creation) of the Somethingness. They are united as members of a category, but they are not united as a single divine spirit being.

The Somethingness is a unity, but He does not unify

the Godhead. The Godhead is a trinity of divine spirits and is not a unity. There is no paradox here. The Godhead paradox is resolved. The mathematical expression of this resolution is: $3 = 3$, $1 \neq 3$, $3 \neq 1$, and $1 = 1$.

9. The Resolution of the Creation Paradox

The Somethingness did replace the nothingness with everything, so how is the creation paradox resolved?

The life-spirit continuum and its constituents of spirits cannot contribute to the resolution of the creation paradox because they exist in zero dimensions. This limit upon the life-spirit continuum disqualifies it from being anything in our world, so it is not a part of the creation paradox.

The part of everything that is not spirit is the natural world and its space-time continuum. The resolution of the creation paradox began with the replacement of the nothingness outside the life-spirit continuum with the space-time continuum. Although the space-time continuum was free of matter and energy before their creation, it had a quantifiable fabric that could time processes governed by natural laws.

The Somethingness, through His Creator spirit interface, created infinite time into the past – eternity. An eternal past could be created after the space-time continuum was created, but not before. Until time was created, the Somethingness and His spirit companions had no past. Time, and therefore the past, was created with the creation of the space-time continuum.

The space-time continuum was created with the quantities of an infinite size and an infinite time into the past. This eternal cause and effect created past applies to everything which exists. This grand circumstance was established during the six days of the creation of the natural world.

When the space-time continuum was filled with its universes, each universe had a created cause and effect past that was eternal. The backward in time cause and effect history of our universe reached back through many collapses and explosions into an eternal past.

The current quantity of the sum of all the matter, energy, and forces of an infinite number of universes, and the fabric of the infinite and eternal space-time continuum has been the same and has existed forever.

The chronology of the Bible indicates the existing crust of the earth is about four thousand three hundred years old. The author of the book of Genesis did not know about the eternal cause and effect history of our world, so he produced the book of Genesis without the knowledge we have today. To him the earth did not have a created past history beyond a little more than two millennia (in his day).

An eternal existence for everything voids the possibility of an origin for the matter, energy, and forces of the creation. When eternity was created for everything, the acts by the Creator that created our world in six days were decreated, but the natural world and the space-time continuum remained. This has made the six days of creation fictitious. (In the life-spirit continuum, the six day creation of everything in our world from nothing is recorded as fact, and this spirit symbol form of information was delivered to the author of the book of Genesis.)

When everything has always existed and there never was an origin for everything, then there never was a situation when there was nothing. If everything never appeared in the place of nothing, then it has never been nothing. Everything never came from nothing. When everything has an eternal cause and effect past, the belief that everything was created from nothing is a fictitious one. The creation of everything from nothing concept was invalidated by the creation of an eternal existence for everything. The method and action used for the creation of everything from nothing has been decreated, so this work by the Creator never happened in our world.

The creation paradox is resolved because everything, in one form or another, has always existed.

The features of the creation paradox are happenings recorded as fact in the life-spirit continuum, but the creation paradox is pure fiction in our world.

The Bible assures us that what is fictitious in our world can be fact in the supernatural world. It also tells us that what was once fact in our world, can be decreated into fiction.

And Jesus looking upon them saith, With men it is impossible, but not with God: for with God all things are possible.
(Mark 10: 27 – KJV)

Appendix A

The Locations of the Creator's Perfections in the Natural World

1. The Presence of Perfection

Faced with the debris of evolution, the knowledge about mutations, the perceived viciousness of natural selection, the evident imperfections of evolved creatures, and the constant threat of disability and death, we wonder: where is the perfection in the Creator's work to be found in the world we live in?

In the moments we dream about a perfect world, sudden violent or corruptive occurrences jerk us out of our reverie and toss us back into a confrontation with our world's imperfections. With ease, we find imperfections in ourselves, our environment, people, and the world. Our reverie was fanciful. Imperfections in our world are inevitable.

We ask: Creator, since you are omnipotent, why didn't you create a world that was free of imperfections? And: Creator, if you created anything perfect, where is it?

He informs us that the perfections He created for our world are hidden within two realms: one that is tangible, and one that is intangible. To us, these perfections are present, but unseen.

After the seventh day of the creation, the tangible and intangible perfections the Creator needed to fulfill His agenda had been created and were in place. But this can mean little to us unless we understand the dynamics of perfection.

Perfection is an absolute. To say, "an absolute perfection", is emphatic, but it is redundant. When we think about something which is described as an absolute perfection, we think the object or action is more than perfect. But there is nothing that is more perfect than what is already perfect. When a condition is perfect, there are no improvements to be had. If there are any improvements to perfection, then the word "perfect" is meaningless. So, "absolute perfection" and "more perfect" are just simple perfection and nothing else. To write and speak otherwise is to communicate nonsense.

Is there such a thing as perfect perfection? No. Perfection is about something other than itself. There is no condition of perfection in which perfection can be perfect with respect to itself. Perfection is a concept, and so, the concept of perfection can have an exact definition, but the perfection of the definition of perfect, beyond what is an exact definition, evades all rational thought.

A condition can be sought which is so complex that perfection will never be attained. In such cases, the effort is to approach a conceptualized perfection without the practical expectation of ever matching the concept with the accomplishment. Here the concept of perfection is a purpose that guides the means.

Perfections are not the same. Perfections vary

according to what they are perfect about. They can be about objects, goals, objectives, and means. The means can be perfect and the goals not; the goals can be perfect and the means not; or they can both be perfect.

There can be one perfection approached by multiple means. The purpose of the various means is to produce the sought perfection.

An artist can have a vision of a perfect graphic representation of what she wants to communicate. Her means may be messy and imperfect, but the near perfect expression of her vision is the purpose of her work. So, the sought perfection projects a purpose into her means. The various means, imperfect as they are, can produce a close approach to the perfection she seeks. In this way, the selected perfection causes a purpose that determines the nature of the means to be used.

An example of the need to use a perfect means to achieve an objective, which is not defined as perfect, is a perfect pass thrown by a quarterback in American football for a score in the corner of the end zone from about thirty-five meters away. The ball has to be thrown so that only the receiver can touch it. The timing must be correct, that is, the ball needs to leave the quarterback's hand so that the ball and the racing receiver arrive at the corner of the end zone at the same time. The receiver should not have to exert any extra effort to catch the ball. To be exact, the trajectory visualized by the quarterback includes the effects of gravity, air resistance, and air movement. The ball needs a perfect spiral to penetrate the air and stay on course.

The purpose of this perfect means is to score a

touchdown. The score is numerically correct, but it is standard and not a part of the perception of what is perfect. So the goal was not perfection, but it was nevertheless a generator of the perfect means.

2. The Nature of the Creator's Agenda

The Creator rejected every other alternative world He could have created. For the fulfillment of His agenda, the creation is perfect. The Creator's omnipotence cannot create any other world that promotes His purposes better than this one. Yet multitudes of people are repulsed by what they experience, and they seek to compensate their misgivings through the pursuit of obvious perfections in their internal and external environments. The hidden animal drives for the avoidance of disorder, the acquisition of security, the lust to control, and the exercise of power, underlie the dynamics of their beliefs and world views. The resultant blind installation and execution of ideologies in our world proceed against the Creator's agenda.

Before the creation of the natural world, the Creator had envisioned alternative utopian (perfect) worlds which were free of chaos and disorder. These perfect worlds operated like mechanical clocks. His control would be absolute. The pure beings who populated these worlds did not need free wills because their world's laws dictated their behavior. The processes of utopian environments advance from disorder, division, and chaos toward order, unification, and a convergent hyperorganized social system. Alternative choices would be naught. The people

of perfect soceieties would function as biological automa-
tions. The kinds of persons who would adapt well to a
utopian world system are control maniacs, perfectionists,
compulsive metaphysicians, dominant religious leaders,
and other fanatics who seek to impose order, unification,
and an enforced conformity on human beings who were
designed to be otherwise (just as the Creator is otherwise). These dominant kinds of persons often develop
visions and write out political and social ideologies that
justify their compulsions.

Utopias, in the hands of human beings, are totalitar-
ian (no free wills allowed), because the laws of utopian
worlds micromanage all behavior to match an idealized
order.

A human being would have created a world she or he
could control, but the Creator is not human. He chose to
create a world that could function beyond His control and
could operate without the force of His will. Nor would
He allow any other spirit being to control any part of His
creation (and warp His agenda).

But, lawless chaos was undesirable. So He instituted
one set of laws to rule the supernatural world, and a
different set of laws to rule the natural world. All of His
creation is ruled by laws.

The Creator sustains the natural world through the
governance of natural laws. The space-time continuum
is the enforcer of these laws. Like Him, the natural world
is independent, autonomous, and self-regulating. The
Creator's constant intervention and micromanagement
are not required.

The proposal made to Himself by the Creator to

create a world that was free of all human perceived imperfections was rejected by Him. A world made with all the perfections demanded by human beings would be a world in which the accomplishment of His agenda would be impossible. The purposes, meanings, and values He seeks require a world that produces the imperfections we perceive around us. These imperfections produce a perfect condition for the fulfillment of the Creator's agenda.

The Creator rejected the installation of any kind of world that would prevent its sentient, self-aware beings from having a likeness to aspects of His mind. He wants His physical beings to have a free will and as many of His other mental attributes mortals can manage. The Creator can identify with such mortals. He can help them, and they can help Him.

3. Tangible Perfections

The natural world is being investigated by thousands of scientists. The investigations of these researchers probe the nature and consistency of our world's foundations and superstructures. To find the Creator's tangible perfections in the configuration of the natural world, we will look first at the superstructures we see around us. The imperfection of the natural world's superstructures increases with the increase of their complexity.

Examples of superstructures are stars, black holes (collapsed giant stars), planets, whales, elephants, people, rabbits, bacteria, viruses, proteins, chemicals, water, atoms, and protons. All of these superstructures are supported by the natural world's foundations, and the foundations are where we will find the Creator's tangible perfections.

To show the connection of the inevitable imperfections found in the superstructures with the Creator's tangible perfections, we will pick a superstructure and increase our focus upon it until we can locate a part of the creation's foundations and the perfection within.

Our selection of a superstructure is a human metastasized (stage four) cancer. From the diseased person's cancer, our first focus is upon one of the cancer cells. From this cancer cell we select one carbon atom and focus again. From the carbon atom we select an electron. We pull this electron out of the atom and set it aside. From the cancer and materials outside the human body, we repeat these steps a trillion times until we have set aside a trillion electrons. We compare all these electrons to each other and to the electron we first selected from the cancer cell.

We soon discover that every electron we examine is identical to every other electron. Their quantitative features are the same when the conditions within and outside them are the same. In addition, we find that under the same influence upon them by matter, energy, and forces, all electrons react in identical patterns of motion and the production of electromagnetic radiation. Electrons are found to be perfect in their essence and existence, and they are perfect in the precision and the manner of their functions. The electron is a tangible perfection in the natural world, and it is but one of the elements of the natural world's foundations.

Scientists have found that all of the fundamental particles of our world are as perfect as the electron in their essence and existence. In their precision and the manner of their functions, they are also perfect. A large part of the natural world's foundations are its perfect fundamental particles.

The rest of the natural world's foundations is the fabric of the space-time continuum, the forces that reach through space, and natural laws. Scientists have found perfection in the precision and the manner with which the forces, and natural laws operate within the fabric of the space-time continuum.

The logic of the mathematics and physics used by technicians and scientists can be related to events in the natural world because of the perfection of its substances and the operations of its foundations.

The nature of the foundations of the natural world has eluded the awareness of priests, prophets, and theologians since the days of animism. Nature's perfect foundations were concealed by its imperfect superstructures. But the perfection in the foundations of the natural world was intimated in the Bible.

> Then the Lord answered Job out of the whirlwind, and said,
> Who is this that darkeneth counsel by words without knowledge?
> Gird up now thy loins like a man; for I will demand of thee, and answer then me.
> Where wast thou when I laid the foundations

of the earth? declare, if thou has understanding.
    Who hath laid the measures thereof, if thou
knowest? or who hath stretched the line
upon it?
    Whereupon are the foundations thereof
fastened? or who laid the corner stone thereof?
    When the morning stars sang together, and
all the sons of God shouted for Joy?
        (Job 38: 1-7 – KJV)

Within the foundations of the earth and the natural world,
"the measures" and the "stretched . . . line" are absolute
in their perfection.
    The connection between the natural world's tangible
perfections and its intangible perfections is process,
a/k/a time. Given an amount of time, superstructures
will be constructed which will have the potential to fulfill
the Creator's agenda.
    Within the cancer cell we selected, we know there is
genetic imperfection – a malignant anomaly. Yet the
foundations that support the existence of the cancer
cell are made of perfect units. Because of its complexity
and its undesirable dynamics, the cancer cell is a good
example of the inevitable imperfections that are produced
when perfect fundamental particles combine to make
superstructures.

4. Perfect Intangibles that Generate Imperfect Intangibles

If the Creator wanted perfect sentient beings who had

the likenesses to Him He seeks, He could have created them in an instant. But this never happened, so we know the Creator planned otherwise. The evidence around us of the inevitable imperfections indicates the recipients of His likenesses will be imperfect.

The natural world's support of these imperfect objectives is analogous to how the intangibles of the organization of the human body/brain combination act as a means to support consciousness.

Any likeness within the character of human beings to some of the aspects of the mind of the Creator will be imperfect because of the biological support mechanisms of the body/brain combination. The mortal creature's mind is one of these imperfect intangibles. These imperfect intangibles are nevertheless an important part of the Creator's agenda.

The intangible likenesses to Him which the Creator wants to see in His sentient creatures is self-awareness, intelligence, effective self-directed free wills, independence, autonomy, the self-confidence to develop value, meaning, and purpose, and the ability to interface well with the natural world and the world of spirits. Within the body/brain combination, all of these likenesses to His inner image will be imperfect intangibles.

These imperfect intangibles are destined to exist in beings throughout the infinite number of universes of the natural world.

The organizational functions of the natural world and the natural world's lawful chaos and disorder are two of the Creator's perfect intangibles. These two intangibles are perfect for being the means to what can be accomplished. Natural law abiding chaos and disorder allow variety and flexibility. Variety and flexibility of action in the natural world are components of a greater perfect intangible.

The greater perfect intangible of the organized functions of the natural world use both perfect and imperfect means in systems of action which will advance the Creator's agenda. In some organized functions, all the means used are imperfect. But, even though the parts of this organized system are imperfect, their coordination is a perfect intangible. The imperfect earthlings are no doubt part of one of these complex kinds of perfect intangibles.

The intangible means within the creation which promote the imperfect intangibles sought by the Creator are perfect for the purposes assigned to them, and they drive the natural world toward the production of sentient creatures who can assist in the fulfillment of His agendas.

Relevant Notes

The mechanisms which implement the Creator's perfect intangibles are generated by elaborate combinations of His tangible perfections.

The positives of human behavior such as contract fulfillment, sensible ethics, honor, love, etc. are included in the list of elements which are a part of His inner likeness. There are more. These likenesses provide beings like us value, meaning, purpose, and significance.

Appendix B

Why the Creator Hides

1. The Free Will Requirement

Simultaneous to the six days of the creation of the natural world, more than a billion years of the history of the evolution of life on earth were created. This combination of creations was the first step of the Creator's trek toward the fulfillment of His agenda. After this step was taken, the earth was populated with self-aware sentient beings that had the potential to have effective free wills. (Of course, they were recreated after Noah's flood.)

Part of the Creator's agenda is to evolve physical beings with whom He can relate. For His relationship with physical beings to be meaningful (to Him), He needs for them to have an effective free will. His interest in relating to sentient beings reaches His highest level when these beings have self-incorporated a likeness to Him to the degree allowed by their internal and external environments.

Such free willed persons can find a way to share in His agenda without giving up their free wills. Persons who are free to have unfettered comprehensive thoughts, and manage their behavior in a constructive way, are those with whom He wants to engage -- so He can end His isolation. These kinds of people are more like Him than any of those that are otherwise.

Those who give up their free wills have chosen to be less like the Creator and more like their indifferent, mindless, material environment. Conformity to ideologies, which require the suspension or rejection of one's free will, reduces people to being equivalent to domesticated animals. The minds of such people are closed.

Those who, albeit unwittingly, impede and thwart the accomplishment of the Creator's purposes are those who demand the surrender or dismissal of free wills. Among the tools used to get people to dismiss their free wills are doctrines, ideologies, institutions, organizations, governments, pain, anger, fear, drugs, and love. The dismissal or surrender of one's free will is what other people want; it is not what the Creator wants. Such disabled wills cannot help the Creator fulfill His agenda.

Minds have effective free wills when they are open and functioning in a context of what is related to what is real.

2. The Reason the Creator Hides

Free wills are impossible when the brain is overwhelmed by stimulus. After the brain's chemistry is exhausted, its mind becomes dysfunctional. Pushed further the mind collapses into a state of disorientation. The repetition of this process breaks the will and the spirit. Emptiness follows. One's identity and integrity are gone.

This is the existential condition we would suffer if the Holy Spirit, God the Father, or the Creator were visible to us everywhere we looked. The Creator's visible presence would overwhelm us. Our personal space, our efforts to control our lives, our efforts to forge a meaningful identity, would alternate between Him and ourselves until we lost control of our lives. Whatever we were as persons would be voided. We would end our lives functioning like pets or draft animals. The existential condition of humanity would be one of abject slavery.

This state of existence and the processes that produce this kind of dysfunctional behavior are not a part of the Creator's internal image. To avoid the destruction of the part of His internal image which He had placed within humanity, the Creator hides Himself.

This is evidence of both His divine wisdom and His divine humility.

You will not detect the Creator within the foundations or the superstructures of the natural world. You will not see His signature imprinted upon stars, planets, or creatures. If you seek Him in the eternal past history of our universe, He will not be there.

Everything (within all the universes of the creation) was created to exist and function as if it had existed for eternity. His creation action decreated its six day beginning. What has had no beginning has had no need for a creator. The Creator decreated the need for any creator. The natural world exists as if He never existed.

The Creator has hidden Himself so well, many believe He does not exist now or at any time backward through eternity.

The Creator's signature on His work will only be found within the intangibles – those unseen things about which we think -- things like an eternal future for the natural world.

Appendix C

The Creation of Death the Facilitator

Outside the garden in Eden, the ecological systems were spread throughout the earth in a mosaic of interlocked wildernesses which had adapted to their terrain, waters, and climate.   Except for the garden, inorganic and biological chaos reigned. Survival and reproduction were the prime motivators. Love was limited to parents for their offspring and members of social groups who shared feelings of belonging to each other.

Death was a certainty for every creature. The multitudes, that were born or hatched, faced predators, rivalries, diseases, accidents, aging, and natural disasters.   The slaughter was rampant. Each species was stalked by an eventual extermination.

Death is a direct product of the operation of the Creator's natural laws.

The Bible gives us a hint about the status of death in the existential condition of human beings and other creatures.

Nevertheless man being in honour abideth not: he is like the beasts that perish.
This their way is their folly: yet their posterity approve their sayings. Selah.

Like sheep they are laid in the grave; death
shall feed on them; and the upright shall have
dominion over them in the morning; and
their beauty shall consume in the grave from
their dwelling.

.   .   .   .

Man that is in honour, and understandeth
not, is like the beasts that perish.
(Psalm 49: 12-14 – KJV)

(Honour is the British spelling for honor. Selah is probably a signal to play music during a pause in the reading
of the psalm.)

The termination of the living is the facilitator of
evolution. When a dominant species fails to adapt to
a sudden change in their environment, its members
are eliminated. Another species, which had mutated
into a more viable kind of creature, filled the vacated
environment. The elimination of the members of one
species ends one step in the process of evolution, and the
spread of the replacement species is the next step.

Although evolution is a meandering process which
produces creatures with brains of various sizes, the members of the replacement species with larger brains had
the ability to use new information not previously appre-
hended by the smaller brained animals. With larger and
more efficient brains, the chances for the survival and the
dominance of the replacement species improved.

Even though a species prevails, the death of each of
its members is guaranteed. Each creature is expendable.
Each creature will die, but the process of evolution and

the advance of the agenda of the Creator continue.

When we choose to measure the value of a human being according to her mass, we discover that to our indifferent universe, an equivalent mass of sand and water is of equal value. The complexity of the chemical processes in the body and brain of the human organism has no more value to the natural world than the simple mindless chemical combinations of two hydrogen atoms with one oxygen atom (to make a molecule of water). To the natural world, the value of a dead human is the same as a live one. The intangibles of well organized matter have no more value than the meaninglessness of disordered matter (when the masses are the same).

In every universe, the worth of value, meaning, and purpose is neither positive nor negative. The worth of these intangibles is neutral. The most concerted search for purpose, meaning, value, and guides to ethics and morality, will never be discovered within the quantitative dynamics of matter, energy, forces, and the fabric of the space-time continuum. Nor will the significance of a creature's essence and existence be found in our world. Everything is neutral in value, meaning, and sense to the natural world.

The Bible recognizes this kind of neutrality in our world by applying the term "flesh" to the physical substance of human beings and other animals. Note the use of this term to describe what Noah loaded onto his ark.

> And of every living thing of all flesh, two of
> every sort shalt thou bring into the ark, to
> keep them alive with thee; they shall be male

and female.

(Genesis 6: 19 – KJV)

Note again how "flesh" is used to describe Adam and Eve and antediluvian mankind.

> And the rib, which the Lord God had taken from the man made he a woman, and brought her unto the man.
> And Adam said, This is now bone of my bones, and flesh of my flesh: she shall be called Woman, because she was taken out of Man.
> Therefore shall a man leave his father and his mother, and shall cleave unto his wife: and they shall be one flesh.
>
> (Genesis 2: 22-24 – KJV)

> And God looked upon the earth, and behold, it was corrupt; for all flesh had corrupted his way upon the earth.
> And God said unto Noah, The end of all flesh is come before me; for the earth is filled with violence through them; and, behold, I will destroy them with the earth.
>
> (Genesis 6: 12, 13 – KJV)

In the Bible the bodies and brains of human beings and all other animals were "flesh", and this "flesh" was made of matter taken from an indifferent universe. "Flesh" inherited the indifference and mindlessness of our universe. Without some kind of conscious intervention by ourselves, our mindless flesh will drag our minds towards insignificance by operating like the rest of the natural world. The Creator planned to evolve brains of flesh which had the capability to intervene within an indifferent environment and produce effects that were benign and/or good. Such interventions, which transcend indifferent natural effects, are necessary to advance the Creator's agenda.

Absent from the universe and its natural laws are the categories of what is good, bad, and evil. Nature's laws have a practical value with respect to the Creator's agenda, but their governance does not include the automatic generation of what is good, bad, and evil. The lack of these values in a quantitative world was necessary to evolve the kinds of creatures the Creator sought to produce.

The physical world had to be unfettered by the constraints of laws that forced automatic good, bad, and evil compulsions. The absence of these ethical and moral compulsions in nature allows self-aware, intelligent creatures to develop independence, autonomy, and free wills – all characteristics of the Creator.

The Bible shows our universe operated this way because it must.

> Doth a fountain send forth at the same place sweet water and bitter?
> Can a fig tree, my brethren, bear olive berries? either a vine, figs? so can no fountain both yield salt water and fresh.
> (James 3: 11, 12 – KJV)

The evidence that shows the indifference and mindlessness of our universe and its natural laws is found in each creature's created cause and effect past history. This created past is backwards in time for eternity. After a creature dies, the matter, energy, and forces in its body have an anticipated eternal cause and effect future.

Death drove the created evolutionary processes of life on earth for at least a billion years of created time. The debris of death (the associated fossil and archeological records in the ground and in museums), guarantees factual support for the creation of evolution in six days.

Appendix D

The Team of Spirits and Mortals

With ease, mortal beings reject the mindlessness of our indifferent universe. To spirit beings (excluding the Creator) a mindless indifferent universe is beyond their understanding and acceptance. So, the two kinds of beings find a common cause in our world through the search for value, meaning, and purpose. Spirits and mortals can cooperate to promote improvements to their existence. The Bible anticipated this kind of teamwork between spirits and people.

> And from Jesus Christ, who is the faithful witness, and the first begotten of the dead, and the prince of the kings of the earth. Unto him that loved us, and washed us from our sins in his own blood.
> And hath made us kings and priests unto God and his Father; to him be glory and dominion for ever and ever. Amen.
> (The Revelation 1: 5, 6 – KJV)

"Kings and priests unto God . . ." are a part of a team made of physical and spirit beings.

Teamwork among spirits and physical beings was in a state of development in the garden in Eden. The project failed, and Adam and Eve were expelled. Since then spirits and human beings have attempted to interact and cooperate. In the Bible, these kinds of interactions were often not teamwork, but instead formed master/slave relationships. By elevating the quality of their behavior, human beings will increase the probability of the formation of teams that include spirits. These special teams will replace the obsolete master/slave relationships among its members.

Appendix E

The Distortion of the Probability of Our Existence
by the Governance of Natural Law

We are here, so the probability of the evolutionary development of self-aware physical beings in our universe is one (one hundred percent). This is because the laws of chance were made irrelevant by the Creator's configuration of matter, energy, and forces, and the enforcement of natural laws by the space-time continuum and its fabric.

All arguments which involve the probability of the existence of life in our universe are in error and therefore can be dismissed. The errors these arguments have is due to the failure to factor into their logic and mathematics the effects natural laws have upon the probability of the development of living beings.

Since we do not understand or know about every natural law, we cannot make accurate calculations about the chances for the existence of sentient creatures in our universe.

We are the product of the creation of billions of years of the operation of natural laws. Once created, these billions of years became the real cause and effect history of our universe. The six days of creation were decreated, so, in our world, the Creator made these six days fictitious. (In the life-spirit continuum, the six days of the creation are recorded as having happened, so this happening is not fictitious there.)

As created, the universe must create sentient physical beings. We are some of these. There are others.

The automatic production of beings like us is necessary to advance the Creator's agenda, so the natural laws He created impose a probability of one (one hundred percent) for our existence.

Appendix F

If Truth Was a Person, He or She Would Never Stop Laughing at Us

1. The Sources of Knowledge

What is true is not the same as its source. With his staff, Moses struck the desert boulder and water poured forth, but the water that filled his gourd was not the same as the rock and the source of water. Understanding what we know improves when we are aware of the nature of the sources of our knowledge.

Our minds identify the directions from which we receive our information. We identify the sources of our information as being from outside our minds or from inside our minds.

Our brain and body sensations are identified as coming from outside our minds. We name the outside source of data: our external environment.

The source of input we identify as originating from inside our minds we name: our internal environment. Our compulsions, addictions, habits, emotional reflexes, reflexive thoughts, and rational thoughts are examples of input that originated from our internal environment. Lodged within our internal environment is an entity we identify as ourselves. This nimble self-identifying entity interprets and manages the internal and external streams of input which occupy its attention.

Part of our external environment is our brain/body combination. We cannot sense any of the trillions of electrical and chemical processes of our physiology and nervous system which produce our feelings, thoughts, perceptions, and sensations within the brain/body combination. What is real in our brain/body combination is outside our consciousness and inaccessible to our minds. The brain/body processes are part of our external environment. These processes are organized by our brains into input to our minds. The inputs into our minds are representations. They are not the processes that made them. Once they enter our minds, they are sorted and identified as relevant to either our external environment or our internal environment.

Lifelong experience with our environments inculcates a mechanism in our minds which judges and selects items of input for rejection or acceptance. The process of interpretation, rejection, and acceptance of delivered data often produces a mind whose symbolic representations of our environments are not aligned with what is real. Through its reflexive impulses, our mind does not mean to deceive us, but often what it tells us is equivalent to lying.

The sources of the data we receive can easily be misidentified. We identify data from our internal environment as coming from our external environment and visa versa. At all times, what we are told by our minds is never the same as what is real. The sources that input our mind's visions of our external environment are what is real. What is real is everything outside our minds. What we claim is reality includes perceptions of the nature of the sources of the data we receive.

2. The Difference between What Is Real and Reality

Reality and what is real are not the same. Reality is what we perceive. What is real is independent from whatever we think or imagine. Reality is dependent upon what is real. If what we think or imagine is independent from what is real, then fantasy, illusion, and delusion are the nature of our thoughts.

We assign the value of truth to what we claim is reality. We know when something is true. Truth is a concept intuitively formed in our minds. The truth is part of reality; it selects elements of our external environment to which we give serious consideration; yet the truth is not the same as its sources. The truth -- the concept – does not exist in the quantitative world outside our minds in any kind of form. The source of the truth does exist outside our minds. The source of the truth is what is real.

We speak of being in touch with reality, but even if we are in touch with reality, this is not the same as being in direct touch with what is real. We cannot be in direct touch with what is real because our apprehension of the features of our external environment is managed by the reality lodged within our minds.

The mind of each person is different from the mind of any other person. This is due to the unique interneuron connections and the unique chemical distribution system of each brain. The brains and minds of identical twins are alike but dissimilar due to their lack of the same location. Their perspectives and emphasis vary when they receive the same data. So our reality is never going to be the same as the reality of another person.

3. Our Mind's Biologically Based Virtual Reality

When we look at a tree, the tree we see inside our minds is not the actual tree. The biology of our brains constructed an image of the tree in our minds. This image is a virtual tree. The tree outside our minds is what is real. The tree inside our minds is a part of the virtual landscape we perceive as the world around us. To be aware of the extreme difference between the virtual tree in our minds and the actual tree in front of our eyes, we have but to note that the virtual tree in our minds is neither dead nor alive, and it has no mass. The image of the tree in our minds has no measurable quantities, but the tree outside our minds can be measured and quantified in many ways. So our virtual reality visions are not quantifiable the way consciousness is not quantifiable.

The degree to which our minds align what we perceive with what is real varies. For the sake of managing our views of reality we will use the simplest possible categorization of the perceptions found within our virtual reality.

There are three categories of virtual facts, (which we perceive within our virtual reality). These categories are ranked according to the degree to which their information can be aligned with what is real. Each category has its own source of information, and these sources are not alike.

The source of first degree virtual facts is data drawn from scientific research, logically disciplined systems of thought, and other analytic disciplines that generate quantified information. The information that is verified by measurable quantities produces our virtual facts of the first degree.

Physics is an example of a source of virtual facts of the first degree. Another example is information about our external environment which is not scientific, but which we can share with others. We can share the knowledge of the existence of a baby with other people. The baby is quantified in the sense that it is one body in one place at one time.

The source of our second degree virtual facts is our internal environment. This source gives us images and symbols that were not determined by any kind of scientific method or logical system of thought. The subject matter is abstract, intuitive, and cannot be quantified. These representations can be repeated and tested for comparison with others, so these virtual facts are part of our virtual reality and the virtual reality of others.

An example of a virtual fact of the second degree is the fact of consciousness (or the fact of the existence of minds). Consciousness cannot be quantified, and its existence in nature cannot be detected by our senses. Consciousness is a state or condition. We know it exists in ourselves and in other people. When we think of consciousness we invent an elaborate constellation of images and symbols which we associate with consciousness. These images and symbols give us a circumstantial basis for accepting the existence of consciousness as a virtual fact which is aligned with what is real. Yet, the information sources are from inside our internal environment. The degree to which we can have confidence in these sources of information is second to quantifiable information, so knowledge about the existence of consciousness is a virtual fact of the second degree.

The third source of information produces virtual facts of the third degree. This source is the life-spirit continuum. Assessing the status of what is supernatural in our virtual reality is similar to the assessment of the status of consciousness within our perception of reality. Like consciousness, the supernatural world has no time or dimension features. Unlike consciousness, in a world of zero dimensions, there is nothing that can be objectively ascertainable the way we ascertain consciousness. The life-spirit continuum does not exist in our quantifiable external environment, and it does not exist in our internal environment. The spirits behind psychic phenomena and supernatural happenings performed by divinity have the same source: the zero dimension life-spirit continuum. The degree to which we can have confidence in the supernatural sources of information is third to quantifiable and objective nonquantifiable information. So, virtual facts about the actions of spirits and the matters of their world are virtual facts of the third degree.

The source of virtual facts of the third degree is separated from us by the supernatural barrier. Beyond the supernatural barrier the facts are ectoreal. (In Greek, "ektos" means "outside". Ecto- is derived from ektos.) The life-spirit continuum's virtual facts of the third degree are part of an ectoreality within the virtual reality of our minds.

Third degree virtual facts in our virtual reality are neither fiction nor fantasy. Fiction and fantasy occur in our external and internal environments, but they do not qualify as any kind of facts. They become part of our virtual reality when we choose to embrace illusions and accept being deluded.

4. Contact by Spirits

For thousands of years, people, prophets, saints, and religious leaders have been contacted by spirits. Jesus was one of them. Jesus, as a human being, taught His followers facts that could be classified within all three degrees of virtual facts. These virtual facts were placed in the minds of His followers under the title of "all things". His disciples were concerned about remembering what they were taught after He was gone, so Jesus told them:

> But the Comforter, which is the Holy Ghost,
> whom the Father will send in my name, he
> shall teach you all things, and bring all things
> to your remembrance, whatsoever I have
> said unto you.
> (John 14: 26 – KJV)

When a person asks the Holy Spirit or any other spirit about what is true, these spirits answer by altering electrical and chemical processes in the brain in order to effect the equivalent of a spoken or read message. Spirits use this method because they have no physical form with which to communicate with people, and the Creator requires their actions to be natural law compliant.

When the Holy Spirit touches us, it alters our physical brain in a way that delivers a message which fits the specific virtual reality we own. The Holy Spirit is part of our ectoreal source of virtual facts of the third degree. Whatever the Holy Spirit said and whatever He placed in the virtual reality of our minds has become third degree virtual reality facts.

The meaning of the message is virtual as well. Often, messages are received and interpreted by minds that are closed. These minds confuse their virtual reality with what is real. It is not possible for the possession of absolute truth to occur in any physical brain. What we believe is an absolute truth is at best a virtual fact, and at worst it is a delusion. Absolutes exist in what is real, but in our minds, what we call absolute is always virtual. Even the Creator in human form would have to use His human biologically based virtual reality to operate as one of us, and perceive what is real in a virtual reality form.

A Relevant Note

The above quotation from the Bible implies that the Holy Spirit cannot teach the followers of Jesus anything which Jesus did not tell them while He was on the earth.

"All things" was qualified by Jesus to mean ". . . whatsoever I have told you".

5. The Solution

Knowing about the sources of the three degrees of virtual facts, and knowing how wrong we can be about what is real, we should not be surprised when the Creator adopts a human form, always incognito, and acts as a teacher to improve our ability to align our virtual reality with what is real.

Cause and effect relationships: Causes are generated by events which preceded them. The causes themselves combine to produce effects which in turn become causes of future effects. The relationships between the causes and the effects are the natural processes which convert the causes into effects. The matter, energy, and forces processes are the connections among actions, reactions, and the relentless advance of our natural world into the future.

Decreate: To create is to produce something which did not exist before. To decreate is to annihilate something which existed. In supernatural happenings, creation can produce something from nothing, so, in this context, the decreation of something is to change something into nothing.

Ectoreal: The Greek word for outside is ektos. The ecto- prefix in ectoreal is derived from this Greek word. Ectoreal refers to all of what is real on the supernatural side of the creation, that is, all that is in the life-spirit continuum (heaven, hell, purgatory, and anything else outside of the natural world).

   Except for a divine intervention, there is never anything which is ectoreal which happens in the natural world.

Ectoreality: This word is derived from ectoreal. Ectoreality is the set of thoughts which represent the happenings of the supernatural world. These representations of the supernatural world are not themselves what they represent. They may be aligned with the things and happenings of the world of spirits, and when they are aligned, they produce an accurated ectoreality of the life spirit continuum and/or a divine intervention in the natural world.

Firmament: The sky, in the daytime and in the nighttime, looks like an upside-down bowl. The ancient cosmologists concluded there did indeed exist an upside-down bowl and its contents which supported everything that existed in the heavens. The source of rain water was believed by the ancients to be a volume of water which was spread over the outside surface of the bowl. The ancient cosmologists believed this construct was held in place by supernatural forces.

Life-Spirit Continuum: The life-spirit continuum is the part of the creation which is separate from the natural world. The location of the supernatural world is in the life-spirit continuum. This world operates according to the laws which govern spirit symbols. (These laws are similar to the laws which govern the functions and interactions of symbols in our minds and the minds of other living creatures.)

    The life-spirit continuum has no cause and effect relationships, no time or process functions, no space or place, and no phenomemological occurrences. The perceptible environment and the happenings of the life-spirit continuum are illusory imitations of the occurrences of the natural world.

Nothingness: The state of nothing is functionless. The state of nothingness has function and is dynamic. Nothing is the lack of something. Nothingness is a state which annihilates physical things, nondivine spirit things, nondivine thoughts within its condition, and reduces divinity from actual to potential. Within the nothingness, nondivine essence and existence are absent, and divine essence and existence are potential. Divine presence within the nothingness becomes concomitant with the nothingness.

Recreate: To recreate is to create something which replaces what has been decreated (annihilated by a divine act). A recreation is a combination of a divine act of the decreation of an item and the creation of the item's replacement. The created replaces the decreated. There is no connection or process which connects the recreated with the decreated -- other than the involved supernatural acts.

Space-Time Continuum Fabric: This is the nonmaterial, nonspirit, nonsupernatural, and nonenergetic substance of the space-time continuum. An example of the action of this fabric is the curvature of space by material and energetic bodies such as the earth and the sun. The manifestation of the space-time continuum fabric is the four forces of nature. These forces are postulated to be changes in the configuration of the fabric by matter and energy. Matter and energy themselves are constructed of these forces. The space-time continuum transfers force between and within material and energetic objects.

Spirit Symbols: These are conscious or nonconscious spirit entities in the life-spirit continuum. They can be called spirit symbol beings. Spirit symbols are the essence and existence of what they symbolize. The absolute essence and existence of everything in the creation is found in the population of the spirit symbols. For example, every tree has a spirit symbol counterpart of itself in the life-spirit continuum which embodies its essence and existence. Just as the symbols which exist in our minds are governed by laws, so also are the spirit symbols of the life-spirit continuum governed by the laws of the life-spirit continuum. These two sets of laws have a multitude of similarities.

Supernatural Barrier: This barrier is of supernatural form and separates the life-spirit continuum from the space-time continuum. The barrier prevents supernatural happenings or influence from invading and interfering with the cause and effect processes of the natural world. The supernatural barrier interfaces with the natural world through its zero dimension points throughout the space-time continuum. The barrier is not needed to block natural events from interferring with activity in the life-spirit continuum because natural occurrences cannot pass through zero dimensions.

Supernatural World: (See life-spirit continuum)

Virtual Facts: All facts are virtual because they represent what they are factual about. They are not the items in space-time about which they convey information.

Virtual Reality: The base of virtual reality in computers is an electronic imitation of the human virtual reality in our minds. The virtual reality in the human mind is biologically based, but it is neverthless a virtual representation of what is sensed and integrated into a system which organizes information. For example, any tree we observe is not itself within our brains. It is represented in our minds by an image symbol.

Our representation of what is real outside our minds is always virtual and is never actually what is real. We convince ourselves we are in touch with reality when our biologically based virtual reality is aligned with what is real.

What Is Real: . . . is everything which exsists outside the thoughts of our minds.

Zero Dimensions: . . . is a point in geometry. A point has no length, width, or height. Within a point there is no process because process takes place only in the three dimensions of our world. A lack of process means there is no time in a point either. (Time only exists where there is some kind of process.) Only the life-spirit continuum can exist in zero dimensions and function in a placeless and timeless (out or this world) manner.

CPSIA information can be obtained at www.ICGtesting.com
Printed in the USA
BVOW021026311212

309363BV00001B/5/P

9 781452 564654